Spotlight On
Amsterdam

Connie Moser

Written by Connie Moser

Published by AA Publishing, a trading name of Automobile Association Developments Limited, whose registered office is Fanum House, Basing View, Basingstoke, Hampshire, RG21 4EA. Registered number 1878835.

Packaged for Automobile Association Developments Limited by IL&FS, New Delhi

A CIP catalogue record for this book is available from the British Library.

ISBN 978-0-7495-5469-9

Colour separation by KDP
Printed and bound in China by Leo Paper Products

A03233
Maps in this title produced from mapping © MAIRDUMONT / Falk Verlag 2007
Transport map © Communicarta Ltd, UK

CONTENTS

Central Amsterdam

Western Canals & Jordaan

Eastern Canals

Museum Quarter

Eastern Docklands & IJ Harbour

Further Afield

AMSTERDAM

Amsterdam…how can this city best be described? Tranquil canals and stately waterside mansions with a variety of impressive gable styles, church towers with chiming carillon bells and market squares make up one part of it. Another aspect, however, verges on the eccentric with a famous red light district, soft drugs, tolerant attitudes, a laidback atmosphere, and entertainment ranging from the eclectic to the electrifying. And of course there is, between the real and imagined, another Amsterdam...

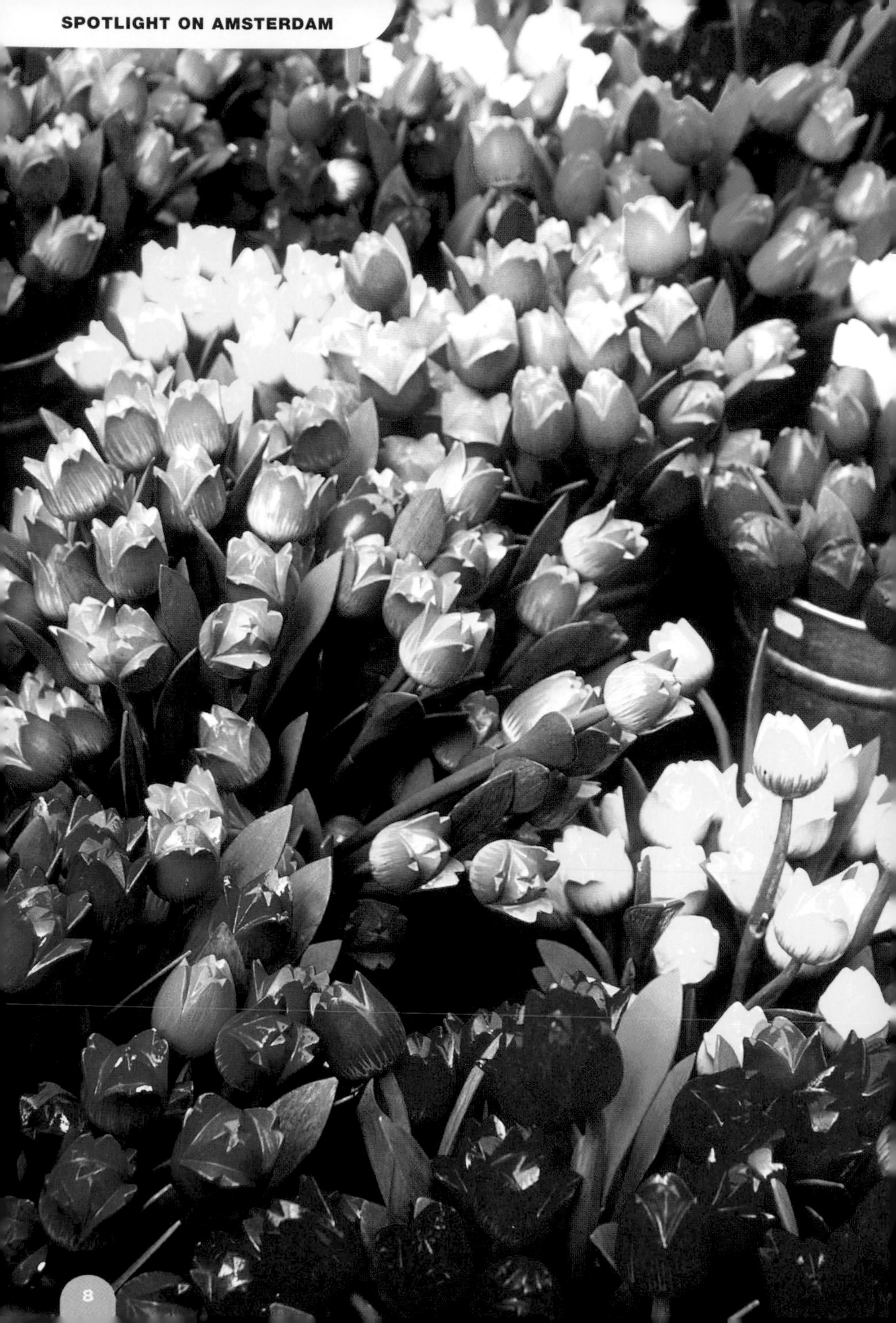

The rich history of Amsterdam has always been connected to water – from the first fishing settlement located on the marshy land at the mouth of the Amstel River, to the pumping windmills used to drain the polders, to the necessity of building and maintaining a system of protective dykes. Bold adventurers crossed the oceans in search of trade and, consequently, the construction of the magnificent canals and stately homes in the 16th and 17th centuries was financed, in part, by the wealth brought to the city by seafaring traders. In its Golden Age the city became the most important trading centre in Europe and the hub of a massive trading empire spanning the globe. As early as the 18th century the city had become a major financial centre and continues to be one. Increased industrialisation moved the city forwards. It has survived Napoleon, two World Wars, internal political conflicts, great fires, intolerance during the Inquisition, famine, disease, deportation and partial destruction. However, Amsterdam continues to change, evolve and integrate, always persevering, experimenting and planning its future.

Nothing short of an adventure is in store when exploring Amsterdam. While this pancake-flat country provides a study in contradictions, Amsterdam is a destination unto itself; emerging as a well-planned city with abundant history, numerous museums, fine dining – from the unpretentious to the exotic. This is a modern city with all the amenities and the reputation of being a place where just about anything goes: liberal laws permit prostitution which has been tolerated since the 17th century; special cafés sell cannabis; it is considered to be Europe's gay capital where same-sex marriages are permitted, as is euthanasia.

Apart from the garish glare of tacky signs and its decidedly seedy side, the city also offers old-world charm, from the elegant to the sublime, with its changing schedule of entertainment and special events, ranging from exhibitions of local and international interest, concerts from classical symphonies to jazz and pop, all kinds of festivals and an abundant nightlife in more than 1,200 cafés and nightclubs. Every day some 40 concerts and theatrical performances take place, around 16,000 annually in 55 theatres and concert halls. There are also 61 cinemas with film selections from around the globe.

Works by renowned artists Rembrandt, Vermeer and Van Gogh along with artworks by other internationally acclaimed artists can be seen in 54 museums.

The flavour of the city today is expressed in a mix of architecture ranging from medieval to contemporary, accented by a variety of offerings from street vendors to open markets and shops selling anything from the wacky to the unique. Its friendly inhabitants comprise a multicultural melting pot of 174 nationalities whose diversity gives the city its international allure. Amsterdam residents are sociable and helpful and most speak several languages. The city is also a dynamic economic powerhouse with many international businesses operating here, as well as the commodities exchange.

The city has the feel of a large village, even though the population is almost 750,000. Amsterdam is compact, easy to get around and well marked. Walking is really the best way to discover the city and a glass-topped canal boat cruise is a good way orientate yourself as it opens up a perspective which you just can't get on land. Amsterdam is a wonderful city to discover – it can be amusing, surprising, shocking, scenic, entertaining, educational and great fun, but it is certainly never dull. Nicknamed the "Venice of the North", the concentric rings of the canals circling out from Centraal Station to Dam square and beyond promise hours of enjoyment and discovery. You can meander from one scenic location to the next, immersing yourself Amsterdam's unique ambience.

Pianola
Museum

De Star Hofje

DE JORDAAN

Zon's Hofje

Tulip
Museum

Huis met de
Hoofden

Egelantiersgracht

Anne
Frankhuis

Herengracht

Oude
Kerk

Westerkerk

Nieuwe Kerk   CENTRUM

WESTERN CANALS
& JORDAAN
56-79

Magna Plaza

Rosse
Buurt

Koninklijk
Paleis

Nationaal
Monument

Madame
Tussaud's

Houseboat
Museum

Amsterdams
Historisch
Museum

CENTRAL
AMSTERDAM
14-55

OUD

Looier Kunst en
Antiekcentrum

Begijnhof

Agnieten
Kapel

Bijbels
Museum

Allard
Pierson
Museum

WEST

De Krijtberg

Muntoren

Rembrandt-
plein

Bloemenmarkt

Paleis van
Justitie

Tuschinski
Theatre

Stadsschouwburg

Leidseplein

FOAM

Holland
Casino

Museum
Van Loon

Rijksmuseum

House of Bols

Coster Diamonds/
Diamant Museum

Van Gogh
Museum

AMSTERDAM
MUSEUM QUARTER
98-117

Vondelpark

Heineken
Experience

Concertgebouw

Albert
Cuypmarkt

OUD-ZUID

Sarphatipark

DE PIJP

10

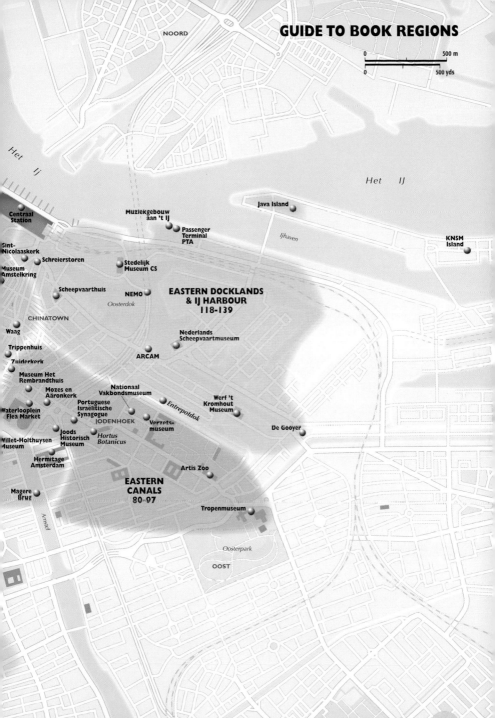

GUIDE TO BOOK REGIONS

500 m

500 yds

NOORD

Het   Ij

Het   IJ

Java Island

KNSM
Island

Centraal
Station

Muziekgebouw
aan 't IJ

Passenger
Terminal
PTA

Sint-
Nicolaaskerk

Schreierstoren

Museum
Amstelkring

Stedelijk
Museum CS

Ijhaven

Scheepvaarthuis

NEMO

Oosterdok

**EASTERN DOCKLANDS
& IJ HARBOUR
118-139**

CHINATOWN

Waag

Nederlands
Scheepvaartmuseum

Trippenhuis

Zuiderkerk

ARCAM

Museum Het
Rembrandthuis

Nationaal
Vakbondsmuseum

Mozes en
Aäronkerk

Waterlooplein
Flea Market

Portuguese
Israëlitische
Synagogue

Entrepotdok

Werf 't
Kromhout
Museum

JODENHOEK

Verzets-
museum

De Gooyer

Joods
Historisch
Museum

*Hortus
Botanicus*

Villet-Holthuysen
Museum

Hermitage
Amsterdam

Artis Zoo

Magere
Brug

**EASTERN
CANALS
80-97**

Amstel

Tropenmuseum

Oosterpark

OOST

11

Central Amsterdam

Central Amsterdam has an atmosphere of its own. First impressions on leaving the busy Centraal Station are of a buzz in the air, masses of people milling or hurrying about, cyclists whizzing by, music from street performers, clanging trams, and a sense of expectation. From the Royal Palace on the Dam to the old Zeedijk with its famed red light district and quirky museums, to hidden churches and Chinatown with its Buddhist temple, or the fragrant floating flower market, there is a fascinating multitude of places to explore. If you like shopping there are some fantastic outlets and shopping centres at Bijenkorf, Kalvertoren, Kalverstraat, Nine Streets and Magna Plaza. Alternatively, you could while away several hours in the wealth of museums such as the magnificent Hermitage or the museum documenting Amsterdam's history, or those dedicated to cats, handbags, the Bible, even marihuana, among other subjects. A relaxing stroll will take you past magnificent 16th- and 17th-century canalside mansions, stately churches and cafés to suit every taste.

CENTRAL AMSTERDAM WALK

1. Nieuwe Kerk
See page 44

Start in Dam square, outside magnificent Gothic Nieuwe Kerk, which is worth a visit. Cross over the Dam, with its obelisk shaped Nationaal Monument in the centre, commemorating those who lost their lives in World War II (page 42). Take Paleisstraat in front of the Royal Palace (page 34) to Nieuwezijds Voorburgwal and turn left.

2. Amsterdams Historisch Museum
See page 24

Further along Nieuwezijds Voorburgwal you will come to the Amsterdams Historisch Museum (housed in a 16th-century converted orphanage) with a wealth of information about the city's history. Continue walking towards the Spui, and turn left for the Begijnhof, a cluster of tiny gabled houses tucked away in a peaceful courtyard.

3. Begijnhof
See page 26

After visiting the Begijnhof and the English Reformed Church continue across the Spui to Singel. Turn right as far as Raamsteeg, then turn left to cross the bridge to Oldspiegelstraat which becomes Wolvenstraat. At Keizersgracht, turn left and walk along the canal to see traditional Dutch pointed, funnel, step and bell-shaped gables.

4. FOAM Fotografiemuseum Amsterdam
See page 32

Continue along Keizersgracht. After the second bridge is a 17th-century mansion that houses a photography museum. Further along Kiezersgracht is De Appel Foundation just off Nieuwe Spiegelstraat. One bridge further along you will come to FOAM Photography Museum (page 32). The Museum Van Loon is across the canal (page 40).

5. Munttoren
See page 39

Turn left onto Vijzelstraat to reach Herengracht and cross the bridge. Turn left along Herengracht past beautiful canal houses. At Leidesstraat turn right to Koningsplein and right again onto Singel, past the Bloemenmarkt (page 28). Emerging again onto Vijzelstraat you can see Muntplein and Munttoren tower. Turn left down Kalverstraat and return to Dam square.

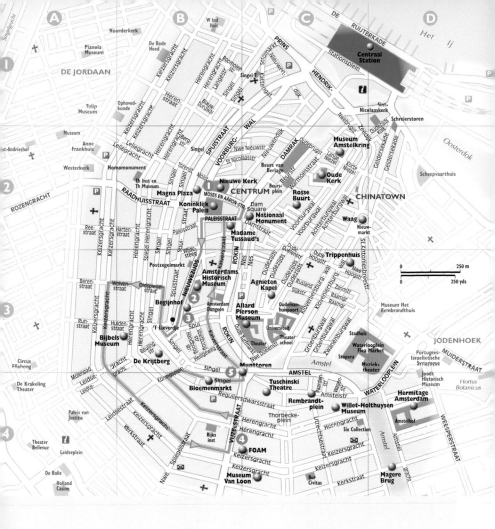

Agnieten Kapel

Once part of the convent of St Agnes (founded in 1397), the Agnieten Kapel or the St Agnes Chapel is part of the Athanaeum Illustre (out of which evolved the University of Amsterdam), the oldest seat of high learning in the city. The current structure was built in the 1470s after the original was reduced to ashes in the great city fire of 1452.

The Agnieten Kapel was founded in an age when Amsterdam had no fewer than 30 convents. Inside these quiet walls and courtyards, secluded from the city life, women of faith would dedicate their life to higher purpose. Nowadays, those entering here are more likely to be dedicating their lives to higher learning. Visitors can enjoy the environs and rest in the lovely inner courtyard garden.

In honour of the 375th anniversary in 2007, the chapel has been renovated. Stonework was cleaned and old passageways alongside the chapel have been converted into glass-covered outdoor areas. Inside, take a seat on one of the college benches in a room filled with 17th-century artefacts, and watch the short video presentation entitled "Athene aan de Amstel" (Athens on the Amstel).

Left: Sunlight falling on the façade of the Agnieten Kapel

Agnieten Kapel

✚ **17 C3**

✉ **Agnieten Kapel**
Oudezijds Voorburgwal 231

☎ 020 525 3377

🖳 **www.uba.uva.nl**

🕒 Mon–Fri 9–5; closed 21–31 Dec and public hols. Exhibition Mon–Fri 10–5, Sat–Sun 1–5

✋ Free

🚋 Tram: 4, 9, 14, 16, 24, 25 Muntplein stop; 1, 2, 5 Koningsplein stop

🚏 51, 53, 54 Nieuwemarkt stop

Allard Pierson Museum

A fine collection of antiquities, fascinating finds and intriguing mummies can be found at the Allard Pierson Museum. The museum is named after the first professor of classical archaeology at the Univesiteit van Amsterdam, who was the founder of this intriguing archaeological cache.

There are more than 16,000 pieces in the collection, most of them contributed by private donors. Exploration around the ancient world produced some fascinating discoveries and this museum is one of the best places to learn about them. The museum features sections on Cyprus, the Near East, the Greek world, Southern Italy and Sicily, Etruria and the Roman World spanning thousands of years of history, with relics and artefacts from each period. The large collection of original Egyptian antiquities takes up the entire first floor and provides a look at some dazzling treasures, along with model pyramids and a computer that can print your name in hieroglyphics.

The Allard Pierson Museum is run in conjunction with the University of Amsterdam's Department of Mediterranean Archaeology. The museum makes Mediterranean Antiquities accessible to scholars and researchers as well as to the general public. Young visitors have their own dedicated displays and programmes. Among the special collections are glass-negative photography slides, and more than 20,000 ancient beads from Africa, Egypt, Rome, Phoenicia, Venice, and Indonesia.

The collection of plaster casts contains in excess of 200 items. Roman copyists used plaster casts during the 2nd century BC to manufacture marble copies of Greek sculptures, and in the 19th century they were used for study purposes.

+ **17 C3**

✉ **Allard Pierson Museum**
Oude Turfmarkt 127

☎ 020 525 2556

🔳 **www.allardpierson museum.nl**

🕐 Tue–Fri 10–5, Sat–Sun 1–5

✋ Inexpensive

🚊 Tram: 4, 9, 16, 24, 25
Muntplein or Spui stops

Above: A visitor admires the Roman plaster cast copy of an ancient Greek statue of Mausollos in the Allard Pierson Museum

Amstelkring Museum

Appearances are often deceptive. What appears from the outside as one of many 17th-century merchant's houses situated along an Amsterdam canal, holds a fascinating secret inside. Upstairs in the loft is a dazzling chapel with a beautifully painted ceiling, pews, altar, an organ and a tiny confessional, with seating for 150 people.

The three upper floors of the house were converted to a secret place of worship known as "Ons' Lieve Heer op Solder" (Our Lord in the Attic) as a result of the Protestant Reformation when life became difficult for Catholics. Churches were whitewashed and stripped of any decoration and convents were closed. When the city converted to Protestantism in 1578, a law aptly named "the Alteration" stated that Catholics could no longer worship in public. Forced into hiding, the Catholics built numerous clandestine churches and chapels, such as this fine example.

When the ban was repealed in the 19th century, most of the hidden churches disappeared. This one, built in 1661, was fortunately preserved in its entirety and

became part of a museum in 1888. There is a fine collection of both religious and secular art along with beautiful sculpture, silver and religious objects.

Situated in the infamous red light district, the Amstelkring is one of Amsterdam's oldest and most remarkable museums. The lower three floors of the house feature 17th- and 19th-century period rooms, all beautifully restored in the original style created by the 17th-century owner,

merchant Jan Hartman. The Parlour, furnished in the Dutch Classical style, gives a glimpse of the opulent lifestyle led by the occupants of the house. The Delft-tiled kitchen, fireplace and black-and-white floor tiles are all original 17th century.

Above: The interior of the light-filled clandestine church, now part of Amsterdam's surprising Amstelkring Museum

✚ **17 C2**

✉ **Amstelkring Museum**
Oudezijds Voorburgwal 40

☎ 020 624 6604

🌐 **www.museumam stelkring.nl**

🕐 Mon–Sat 10–5, Sun and public hols 1–5

✋ Moderate

🚊 Tram: 4, 9, 16, 24, 25 Dam stop

Amsterdam Historisch Museum

The rich and varied history of Amsterdam occupies a former children's home built in the 17th century. The focus is largely on the 17th century and the trades that made Amsterdam the richest city in the world at the height of its Golden Age.

The original children's home on the site dated from 1579, part of St Lucy's Convent, and was demolished when the current orphanage building was constructed in the 17th century. The building had been in use as a home for children until the 20th century. In 1975 the Amsterdam Historisch Museum moved into the premises.

Paintings by well-known Dutch artists, including Rembrandt, portray the history of Amsterdam, including an interesting display of 14 portraits of the Civic Guard protected by a glass enclosure. The entire collection of paintings spans several centuries, styles and historical periods. The original carillon bells that once hung in the Munt Tower are also displayed here, as are suits of armour and old maps of the world, dating back to the early period of exploration. Over the entrance gate, off Kalverstraat, is a carving of orphan boys.

The Governors' room where the governors or regents held their meetings from 1634 until 1960 still exists and is open to the public. During the museum's renovation in the 1960s the room was refurbished in order to re-create a classical 17th-century atmosphere. The splendid painted ceiling was also fully restored.

Prominent group portraits have hung here since the 17th century. There is also a fine collection of engravings. Special exhibitions are held periodically throughout the year.

The growth of the city from the period 1000 to 2000 is explained by interesting map and video displays. The museum houses collections from the 1400s to the present day, some of which are on loan from the Rijksmuseum.

The history of Amsterdam is also imaginatively reconstructed through the museum's excellent collections which include, among others: Pilgrims' tokens, silver artefacts, glassware, jewellery, clothing and shoes, ship and shipbuilding models, porcelain, statues and other items belonging to the city's residents over the past six centuries.

The Amsterdams Historisch Museum also has a dynamic online E-museum with programmes containing a resource of hundreds of photos along with fragments of historic film and documentaries from the Dutch archives on a wide range of subjects such as the 30 Amsterdam districts, fashion and transport in bygone eras.

For more than 200 years the orphanage on this site was the focus of processions held in honour of the Miracle of Amsterdam. When a dying man received the last rites from a priest, the man was sick and his vomit was thrown into the fire, but the communion wafer did not burn. The man was healed and the house was declared a miracle site where a chapel was later built. Pilgrims came from all over Europe to this shrine. After the Reformation, the wafer was relegated to a wooden chest and placed in the attic of the orphanage.

✚ **17 B3**

✉ **Amsterdam Historisch Museum**
Nieuwezijds Voorburgwal 357 and Kalverstraat 92

☎ 020 523 1822

www.ahm.nl

🕐 Mon–Fri 10–5, Sat–Sun 11–5

✋ Moderate

🚌 Tram: 1, 2, 5 Spui stop; 4, 9, 14, 16, 24, 25 Rokin stop

Begijnhof

The Begijnhof, although centrally located in one of the busiest shopping areas on the Spui, offers an unexpected oasis of rest and tranquillity. In 1346, a group of pious lay women came to Amsterdam to form a religious community. The Beguines, as they were called, built the 164 small houses here instead of living in a convent.

The Beguines lived and worked as nuns, but had not taken vows. Rules were

🕀 **17 B3**

✉ **Begijnhof**
Entrances on Spui and Gedempte Begijnensloot

☎ 020 622 1918

📶 **www.begijnhof
amsterdam.nl**

🕓 Mon 1–6:30, Tue–Fri 9–6:30, Sat–Sun 9–6. Services in English on Sun

🎫 Free

🚊 Tram: 1, 2, 4, 5, 9, 13, 16, 17, 24 Spui stop

strict: be of a sober manner, dress and live simply, and receive no male company at night. The women engaged in charitable works and were not permitted to spend the night away from their Begijnhof home.

In 1578 during the Reformation their church was confiscated and turned over to the English Reformed (Presbyterian) Community in 1607. Public displays of Catholicism were forbidden, so the lay sisters worshipped in secrecy, meeting in different houses. Two adjoining houses were purchased and converted into a permanent hidden place of worship in 1655. The unobtrusive structure

opposite the English Church is still a Catholic Chapel. The Houten Huis, or the Wooden House at No. 34, is reputedly the oldest house in Amsterdam (1475).

The English Church at the southern end of the Begijnhof courtyard was originally dedicated in 1419, though it was reconstructed in a more elaborate style after the fires in 1421 and 1452. The Union Jack, Scottish Church and House of Orange flags are displayed here. The Pilgrim Fathers Society presented the American flag and the stained-glass window over the choir exit.

Above: Begijnhof is home to a number of buildings preserved in their original styles

Displays inside the museum showing bibles and religious displays.

De bijbel voor velen

Oude vertalingen van de bijbel

Erasmus en Luther: vertalen uit de grondtalen

De eerste gedrukte
bijbel in de Nederlanden

Bijbels Museum

The Biblical Museum is where the Bible, art and culture meet in a monument full of history. The renowned architect Philips Vingboons built the two historic buildings on Herengracht for merchant Jacob Cromhout in 1662.

This atmospheric setting provides a home for the unique collection of one of the Netherlands' oldest museums, with its well-preserved kitchen, ceilings painted with mythological figures, and a large garden.

Displays include archaeological finds, old bibles dating from the 15th century, and models of ancient temples. There are various artefacts from ancient Egypt, centuries-old models of the temple of Solomon and Herod, and religious objects from the Judeo-Christian tradition.

A 19th-century model of the Tabernacle shows a reconstruction of the sacred shrine housing the Ark of the Covenant. Clay tablets, fragments of papyrus and archaeological remains tell the fascinating story of how the Bible came into existence, and the influence it has had on Dutch society through the ages. Displays centred on a model of the Temple Mount in Jerusalem explain the significance of this sacred place in Judaism, Christianity and Islam.

The collection of bibles includes the first book to be printed in the Netherlands, the treasured Delft Bible, in 1477, and a first edition of the 1637 Dutch Authorised Version. The translation, printing and distribution of bibles have a history which is closely interwoven with the birth and development of the Netherlands as an independent state and also with the evolution of the Dutch language.

Above: Displays of printed bibles inside the atmospheric setting of the Bijbels Museum

⊕ **17 B3**

✉ **Bijbels Museum**
Herengracht 366–368

☎ 020 624 2436

🌐 **www.bijbelsmuseum.nl**

🕐 Mon–Sat 10–5, Sun 11–5; closed 1 Jan, 30 Apr

✋ Moderate, children under 12 free

🚋 Tram: 1, 2, 5 Spui stop

Bloemenmarkt

A brilliant kaleidoscope of colourful seasonal flowers and blooming plants is showcased in Amsterdam's fragrant Bloemenmarkt. The city's floating flower market is a horticultural delight.

Located on the Singel canal between Koningsplein and Muntplein, the Bloemenmarkt is a favourite spot for photographers and souvenir hunters. Amsterdam had more than 20 floating markets in the 17th and 18th centuries.

In those days nurserymen would sail along the city's canals and sell their wares directly from their boats. Nowadays the market is still floating, though the stalls are permanently moored, and the flowers and plants are brought in by truck from the flower market in Aalsmeer. Packets of seeds, bulbs, shrubs, herbs and pots are on sale for gardening enthusiasts.

Above: A stall owner surrounded by an array of colourful cut flowers at Bloemenmarkt

The Netherlands is synonymous with flowers, especially tulips, which were first introduced in the 1600s by Dutch diplomats returning from Turkey. When a Leiden botanist discovered how to change their shapes and colours, tulip cultivation became a national rage with prices reaching astronomical proportions – a single bulb could cost a year's salary or more. By 1637 the bottom fell out of the market and many fortunes were lost.

More than 16,000ha (39,540 acres) are used for cultivating bulbs and flowers. In the spring, a train ride to The Hague will take you through glorious bulb fields in bloom. Or, to be really in the midst of a floral paradise, hire a bicycle and ride through the fields.

✚ 17 B4

✉ Bloemenmarkt
Singel next to Munttoren

🕐 Mon–Sat 9–5:30,
Sun 11–5:30

✋ Free

🚋 Tram: 1, 2, 5 Koningsplein
stop; 4, 9, 14, 16, 24, 25
Muntplein stop

⛴ Museum boat stop 4

Centraal Station

The ornate façade of this Dutch neo-Renaissance style railway station with its distinctive twin towers is an architectural highlight. Constructed on three man-made islands, the building rests on 8,687 piles to keep it stable on Amsterdam's shifting mud and sand.

Built in 1889 by P J H Cuypers and A L van Gendt, the red stone exterior is decorated in Gothic style with carvings, mosaic tiles and gold accents. Two majestic towers guard the entrance: the western tower bears a weather vane while the eastern tower carries a clock.

Controversial when built, as it effectively cuts off the city from its own waterfront, the building was considered by some, particularly the Protestants, to be too decorative (or Catholic, in their view) in its Gothic embellishments, earning the building its nickname, the "French Convent". Cuypers also designed the Rijksmuseum, which stands like a mirror image on the other side of the city and came to be referred to locally as the "Bishop's House".

Centraal Station is the bustling central hub of activity in the city, enlarged many times to cope with increasing demands for travel. Just about every destination in the country and beyond can be reached from here, with some 1,500 trains arriving and departing every day. Easy access to Schiphol airport provides a convenient link for travellers. It is also the hub of tram and bus services, as well as a terminus of the metro system. Behind the station ferries traverse the IJ River, connecting travellers across the water.

Platform 2 has a small VVV tourist office, the main one is across Stationsplein in the white building. The Eerste Class restaurant with its belle époque decor and 19th-century café provides a quiet respite and delicious food. In the main hall below are numerous fast-food outlets and shops.

✚ **17 C1**

✉ **Centraal Station**
Stationsplein

🕐 Daily

🚊 Tram: 1, 2, 4, 5, 9, 13, 17, 20, 24, 25

Above: Tourists and travellers congregate in bustling Centraal Station

FOAM Fotografiemuseum Amsterdam

Both Dutch and international photographers are showcased here in a 150-year-old canalside house. The multifloor gallery space houses exhibitions that change every two to four months.

Large windows let ample light into the exhibition space while the stark walls and modern chrome and glass architectural details serve to create an ambience that does justice to the works displayed. Exhibitions of all genres of photography are held here: fine art, documentary, historical and contemporary including prints and multimedia works. The work of up-and-coming young talent is presented in small, short-term shows alongside large exhibitions of established, world famous photographers. On the last Thursday of the month museum guides give a free tour and explain the pieces on display.

MTV and FOAM have joined hands to encourage young talent by producing an annual show featuring new work.

Above: Displays at the FOAM Photography Museum, an up-to-the-minute gallery in a lovely canalside setting

There is a library of photography books on the upper level, a small café downstairs and a gift shop selling photo-related items and books.

FOAM also publishes a highly acclaimed international photography magazine, available quarterly by subscription. The *Foam Magazine* complements the exhibition, embracing all aspects of photography from historic to avant garde. Each issue is centred around a specific theme and showcases six diverse 16-page portfolios of featured photographers.

- ✚ **17 C4**
- ✉ **FOAM Fotografiemuseum Amsterdam** Keizersgracht 609
- ☎ 020 551 6500
- ᴡᴡᴡ **www.foam.nl**
- ◑ Daily 10–6 (also Thu and Fri 10–9); closed 1 Jan, 30 Apr
- ✋ Moderate, children under 12 free
- 🚋 Tram: 16, 24, 25 Keizersgracht stop

The Hermitage Amsterdam

The city's long and abiding interest in Russian culture and art was hallmarked by the opening of The Hermitage Amsterdam in 2004. Some of the finest collections from St Petersburg's Hermitage Museum in Russia are on loan and exhibited here.

Part of the 17th-century Amstelhof complex on the banks of the Amstel river, the Neerlandia building is a fine example of classic monumental architecture. The first and second floors each house three exhibition galleries. An educational studio or Children's Hermitage is planned for the attic space.

The history of Russia and the Netherlands is inextricably tied. Catherine the Great, who reigned from 1762 to 1796, was an avid collector, purchasing some 4,000 paintings, thousands of drawings and engravings. She also commissioned pieces in silver and porcelain, furniture and decorative arts.

In 1697 the 25-year-old Russian Tsar, Peter the Great, was in Zaandam (north of Amsterdam) to study famed Dutch shipbuilding techniques. When he returned to St Petersburg he had the city laid out with beautiful canals similar to those that so impressed him in Amsterdam. On his study trip in 1697 he picked up more than just boat building tips; he also managed to take home "my little Dutchmen" as he referred to his collection of small canvases painted by the Dutch Masters. Relations were good between the House of Orange and Peter's family, the Romanovs. Anna Paulownia, the wife of Dutch King Willem II, was the sister of Tsar Alexander I.

Above: Outside the Hermitage, the Magere Brug (Skinny Bridge) and Blauwe Brug (Blue Bridge) can be seen crossing the Amstel river

🕂 **17 D4**

✉ **The Hermitage Amsterdam**
Nieuwe Herengracht 14

☎ 020 530 87 55

🌐 **www.hermitage.nl**

🕐 31 Mar–15 Sep, daily 10–5; closed 30 Apr

✋ Moderate

🚊 Tram: 4 Rembrandtplein stop 9 Waterlooplein

🚏 51, 52, 53 Waterlooplein stop

Koninklijk Paleis

At the time when the Koninklijk Paleis or Royal Palace was built (1648–1655), the city's residents described it as the eighth wonder of the world. This grand structure was not designed to be a palace; it was built as a city hall in the period after the Eighty Years War with Spain when Amsterdam was establishing itself as one the world's great cities.

The building was intended to reflect Amsterdam's growing economic and

✚ **17 B2**

✉ **Koninklijk Paleis**
Koninklijk Paleis

☎ 020 624 8698

🌐 **www.koninklijkhuis.nl**

🕐 Closed for renovations until 2009

🚊 Tram: 1, 2, 4, 5, 9, 14, 16, 17, 24, 25 Dam stop

political importance and the city's mood of confidence. It became a Royal Palace in 1808 when Napoleon presented his brother Louis with the title, King of Holland. Louis incurred his brother's wrath for protecting Holland's interests; in 1810 Napoleon sent in troops and Louis fled, leaving his furniture behind. Since then, no one from the Dutch Royal Family has ever lived in the palace. Today, the Royal Family lives in The Hague, but this building is still used for entertaining, official functions, the Queen's New Year receptions and state visits.

The building rests on 13,659 wooden piles. The most impressive room is

the huge Burgerzaal, a vast assembly room extending the entire length of the building. Its design was based on the assembly halls of ancient Rome and contains epic sculptures by Quellian. The beautiful marble floor is inlaid with maps of the eastern and western hemispheres depicting the world as it was known at that time. The 30m (95-feet) high ceiling gives the hall a majestic ambience. Truly palatial throughout, the building's spacious rooms, wall murals, numerous paintings and statues are truly impressive.

Above: The Koninklijk Paleis in Dam square

De Krijtberg

De Krijtberg replaced the original Franciscus Xaveriuskerk, a former clandestine Jesuit chapel, used for worship and prayer since 1654. The church was named after one of the founding Jesuit priests, St Francis Xavier. The nickname "De Krijtberg" (Chalk Hill) was taken from its site on a former chalk merchant's house.

This impressive, neo-Gothic church with its two soaring spires was designed by Alfred Tepe, who had to squeeze the structure between existing buildings on a site where there were three different houses.

Built in 1881, the church was dedicated to worship in 1883. The presbytery beside the church is constructed on the site of two houses, one of which had previously belonged to a chalk merchant. The building is wider to the rear than at the front, incorporating the space that was originally taken up by two of the gardens that existed here.

The interior is ornate, with brilliant towering stained-glass windows, brightly coloured walls and abundant gold decoration. Statues of St Ignatius Lyola, founder of the Jesuit Order, and St Francis Xavier, grace the sides of the high altar in the nave. The church also has an 18th-century wooden statue that was originally housed in the hidden chapel of the Immaculate Conception, depicting the Virgin Mary trampling the serpent.

The presence of a church named after St Francis Xavier attests to the turbulent time when Spain and the Counter Reformation movement held sway over Amsterdam. In fact, Amsterdam remained Catholic choosing not to side with Protestant Prince William of Orange, leader of the Dutch revolt against Spain, until the time when it became obvious that Spain was losing. It was only when Prince William's forces surrounded Amsterdam in 1578, that the city prudently switched sides – a process known as the Alteration.

By the 1630s, Catholic city officials had been replaced by Protestant merchants and the city's churches became Calvinist. A Catholic minority was quietly tolerated but barred from public office. Clandestine attic churches and chapels appeared, even though for the next 200 years Catholic worship was officially prohibited.

The current structure was built in the period of relative prosperity, at a time when the opening of the Noordzee Kanaal (North Sea Canal)

revived Amsterdam's flagging port which had declined following the Napoleonic Wars. Amsterdam was once again free to prosper in the new age of widespread and progressive economic and social development.

Weekday services in Dutch are held (Mon–Fri at 12:30pm and 5:45pm. On Saturday there are services at 12:30pm and 5:15pm. Sunday services include High Mass at 9:30am, Latin Mass at 11am, a mass at 12:30pm without singing, and at 5:15pm with cantor and singing.

✚ **17 B3**

✉ **De Krijtberg**
Singel 448

☎ 020 623 1923

🖳 **www.krijtberg.nl**

🕒 Tue, Wed, Thu and Sun 1:30–5

✋ Free

🚌 Tram: 1, 2, 5 Koningsplein stop

Madame Tussaud's Amsterdam

Astonishingly life-size and life-like state-of-the-art wax figures are admired daily at the Amsterdam branch Madame Tussaud's, where you can see, face to face, famous Dutch and foreign personalities from past and present, and well-known celebrities. The technical special effects are quite amazing.

Among the inhabitants of this waxen world are historical figures – Dutch painters, artists, sportspeople, musicians, fashion models and many more, such as the Dutch Royal Family, Bill Clinton, Winston Churchill, Nelson Mandela, Mahatma Gandhi, Van Gogh, Tina Turner, Michael Jackson and the Dalai Lama to name but a few. You are welcome to photograph and be photographed with them.

One exhibit looks back 300 years to Holland's Golden Age in the 17th-century. Beggars, rat catchers and merchants ply their trades by an old canal. On hand are Rembrandt, Peter Stuyvesant and others.

Madame Tussaud's has been making wax models for more than 200 years. It all started in the 1770s when the young Marie Grosholz – later to be known as Madame Tussaud – learned the art of wax modelling from a Parisian doctor, Philippe Curitis. After inheriting his collection of wax figures, she spent the next 33 years taking the show on the road. The collection has survived shipwreck, fire and World War II bombing. The Chamber of Horrors is a particular favourite. Madame Tussaud's collection has been voted one of Amsterdam's most popular visitor attractions.

Below: Models of a member of the 17th-century Dutch royalty and her maid, dressed in period costume

✚ **17 B2**

✉ **Madame Tussaud's Amsterdam**
Dam 20

☎ 020 523 0623

▓ **www.madame tussauds.nl**

🕐 Daily 10–5:30

💰 Expensive

🚋 Tram: 1, 2, 4, 5, 9, 14, 16, 17, 24, 25 Dam stop

Magere Brug

There are more than 1,200 bridges in Amsterdam, the most famous of which is undoubtedly the white drawbridge, Magere Brug, over the Amstel between Prinsengracht and Keizersgracht, just opposite the Carré Theatre.

The Magere Brug is known as "Skinny Bridge" because of its thin, delicate shape, (*mager* means skinny in Dutch). However, another story has it that two sisters named Magere who lived on opposite sides of the Amstel river had a small footbridge built in 1671 to make visiting each other easier, although the narrow bridge made it difficult for two pedestrians to pass one another.

The style of the current structure is a wooden double-leaf drawbridge from 1840. The bridge master raises the bridge every 20 minutes or so for boat traffic. As the river became busier, a wider bridge was built, and subsequently rebuilt in 1871 and 1929. The current bridge from 1969 is made of dense African azobe wood and is still in use for foot and bicycle traffic. At night it is illuminated and its reflection sparkles in the waters of the Amstel river below. This is perhaps the most photographed and painted bridge in Amsterdam.

Left: Cyclists and pedestrians crossing the Magere Brug

✚ **17 D4**

✉ **Magere Brug**
Between Prinsengracht and Keizersgracht over Amstel river

✋ Free

🚌 Tram: 4 Rembrandtplein stop, 9 Waterlooplein stop

🚇 51, 52, 53 Waterlooplein stop

Magna Plaza

Just behind the Royal Palace on the Dam is Magna Plaza, a massive 19th-century neo-Gothic building. It was originally built as the city's main post office in 1899, but has been preserved and is now an attractive shopping mall, open seven days a week.

Designed by Dutch architect P C Peters, the building combines Roman and Gothic elements. It was built during the days when Amsterdam was experiencing a major construction boom, another famous Dutch architect Petrus J H Cuypers having just completed the construction of both the Rijksmuseum (1885) and the Centraal Station (1889).

Magna Plaza is built on 4,560 piles with an additional 500 added during renovations in 1991.

During the original construction, people in the Jordaan neighbourhood had nicknamed the building "Pear Borough" due to the pear-shaped crowns gracing the top of the building, while others referred to the ornamental style with some sarcasm as "Post-Office Gothic". The 20th-century renovations were carefully executed, preserving the exterior symmetry while adapting the internal structure. A spacious atmosphere was created, adding a glass-domed roof to allow daylight to stream into the atrium, which hosts live music and themed events.

Magna Plaza offers the usual wide range of world brands as well as Dutch products in 40 shops. You can browse outlets over four floors, and overseas visitors can take advantage of tax-free shopping. The interior walkways look down over the central plaza. For refreshments try the Italian-style brasserie, Café Ovidius, or Italian coffee bar Ristretto.

Below: The Dutch Renaissance striped façade of Magna Plaza

+ **17 B2**

✉ **Magna Plaza**
Nieuwezijds Voorburgwal 182

▨ **www.magnaplaza.nl**

🕐 Mon 11–7, Tue–Sat 10–7 (also Thu 10–9), Sun noon–7

✋ Free

🚌 21, 170, 171, 172

Munttoren

The Munttoren or Munt (Mint Tower) stands on busy Muntplein square, at the end of Rokin, and close to Bloemenmarkt flower market and Kalverstraat shopping street. Originally, the tower was part of Regulierspoort, one of the main gates in Amsterdam's medieval city wall. Built between 1480 and 1487, it consisted of two towers and a guard house.

After a fire in 1618 the tower was rebuilt (1619–1620) in Amsterdam Renaissance style. It features an eight-sided tower and an elegant, lead-covered, open spire designed by Hendrick de Keyser, and four clock faces and a carillon of bells made by the brothers Pieter and François Hemony in 1650. An underpass was added to the building during a 1938–1939 renovation.

In 1873, the bells were sold for scrap iron, but were rescued and are now on display in the Amsterdam Historical Museum. The current carillon has 38 bells (11 more than the original), and chime mechanically every quarter of an hour. On Fridays, between noon and 1pm, a carillon player gives a concert on the bells.

The tower was used to mint coins in the 17th century. During the Rampjaar (disastrous year) of 1672, when both England and France declared war on the Dutch Republic and French troops occupied the Netherlands, silver and gold could no longer be safely transported to Dordrecht and Enkhuizen (where coins were minted), and the guard house of the Munttoren was used temporarily to mint coins.

To prevent it from sagging, the Munttoren's foundations are to be renewed during construction of the Noord/Zuidlijn, the new metro line. The city has allocated 1.9 million for this purpose, according to a report in the newspaper *Het Parool* (17 May 2006).

Right: Mint Tower, topped by a weather vane

---

 17 C3

 Munttoren
Muntplein

⏰ Daily. Carillon concert Fri noon–1

✋ Free

🚊 Tram: 4, 9, 14, 16, 24, 25 Muntplein stop

Museum Van Loon

The Van Loon Museum is an elegant canal-side mansion. Built in 1671, its first resident was Ferdinand Bol, a famous Dutch painter and one of Rembrandt's students. The double-sized canal house has 17th- and 18th-century furnishings, family portraits and a lovely formal garden.

Both the richly decorated period rooms and the building's exterior have remained virtually intact and unchanged, which makes for a fascinating historical tour de force. The Van Loon family occupied the house in the 19th century. Several family members held prominent positions as Amsterdam regents and city-mayors, and in the Dutch United East India Company.

Thora van Loon-Egidius, the last resident of the family to occupy the house, was Dame du Palais for Queen Wilhelmina for 40 years, and invited many important royal guests to the Van Loon residence. She died in 1945, and in 1973 the house was turned into a museum.

A fine collection of 80 family portraits is the highlight of the collection at the museum. The earliest of these date from the 16th century and together they portray generations of the Van Loon family, which traces its origins to Loon op Zand, a village near Den Bosch, though their fortunes closely followed that of their adopted city, Amsterdam.

There are also signed furniture, silver and porcelain items from the 18th century and beautifully furnished period rooms, all giving an idea of the opulent Amsterdam lifestyle of an upper-class household during those times. The table in the dining room is laid ready for the host and his guests to be seated, and the Blue Drawing Room and the Red Gent's Room are filled with beautiful objects, as if expecting guests to walk in at any moment. The museum sometimes leases the premises for lectures and meetings.

Behind the house is a wonderfully spacious garden that provides a quiet retreat from the noise of the city, and a coach house. In the 17th century such a large garden behind a canal house was quite unusual, since there were strict zoning laws regulating how deep plots for houses and extensions could be.

The house itself is a typical canal house with the kitchen in the basement, reception rooms on the elevated ground floor, bedrooms on the second floor and the servant's quarters in the top attic.

Parts of the house still remain closed to visitors and, although the owners do not reside in the house, you may sometimes catch a glimpse of their relatives or friends making their way through the museum to their private quarters.

Left: One of the lavishly decorated period rooms in Museum Van Loon

17 C4

✉ **Museum Van Loon**
Keizersgracht 672

☎ 020 624 5255

🌐 **www.museumvanloon.nl**

🕐 Wed–Mon 11–5

✋ Moderate

🚊 Tram: 16, 24, 25 Keizersgracht stop

Nationaal Monument, Dam Square

Due south of Centraal Station via Damrak is the Dam National Monument, erected in remembrance of those who died during World War II. A tall, white, conical sculpture, it is a popular spot for people to congregate. The monument was unveiled on 4 May 1956.

Each year on 4 May, known as Nationale Dodenherdenking (National Memorial Day), dignitaries, including representatives of the Royal Family, gather at the monument to commemorate the victims of World War II and other military conflicts such as peacekeeping missions in Lebanon and Bosnia.

The Dam has always been the centre of the city. The name originates from the 13th century when residents built a dam here to protect their homes from the Amstel floods, hence also the name of the city. There was a time when the Amstel river flowed where the monument now stands and boats would dock here to unload their cargo for the markets and weigh houses on the square. The Amstel has since been filled in and the markets have moved to other locations in the city.

The Dam as it exists today grew out of what were originally two squares: the actual dam, called Middledam, and Plaetse, an adjacent plaza to the west. The area became a centre not only of commercial activity but also of government and is the site of Amsterdam's town hall.

The Weigh House was torn down by King Louis Bonaparte in 1808 because it blocked his view from the Palace. Bonaparte ruled the Netherlands as the King between 1806 and 1810.

The Dam has also been the site of political and military events, from grand parades of military might to royal processions. Protests on the Dam include the Anabaptists' riots in 1535, a revolt over loot from the silver fleet a century later, and protests against decreased employment benefits in 1935 which led to widespread workers' revolts. Innocent citizens were executed here towards the end of World War II. In the Vietnam era it was the scene of anti-war demonstrations, and also the venue for student unrest and protest. In 1980, the investiture of HRH Queen Beatrix caused riots. There have been silent vigils and noisy gatherings ever since.

On 2 February 2002, Dutch Crown prince Willem Alexander and Máxima Zorreguieta from Argentina married in the Nieuwe Kerk on the Dam with great fanfare and celebration.

The monument itself, was designed by J J P Oud. Conical in shape, it is about 200m (656 feet) tall, and includes 11 urns that contain soil from the cemetries of the 11 former Dutch provinces.

Over the course of the centuries, Amsterdam's main square became a "national" square well known to nearly everyone in the Netherlands.

Right: The Nationaal Monument is a popular meeting place

✚ **17 C2**

✉ **Nationaal Monument, Dam**

🕐 24 hours

🚉 Centraal Station

Nieuwe Kerk

Nieuwe Kerk is located in the middle of the city centre at Dam square next to the Royal Palace. This monumental Gothic church – the second church to be built in the city – dates from 1408. In January 1645 a fire destroyed its interior, which was fortunately restored by talented artists and artisans of the period, the Dutch "Golden Age".

Originally a Roman Catholic church, it later became part of the Dutch Reformed Church. Today, it is managed by a private trust, and is famous for its much talked-about, large-scale exhibitions showcasing treasures from many different countries, cultures and religions. The church is one of the most visited exhibition locations in the Netherlands.

There is no altar; in its place is the elaborate monument-tomb of one of the Netherlands' heroes, Admiral de Ruyter.

Two more features are particularly noteworthy. The organ, one of the most beautiful in Europe, is used for concerts and special musical services on Sundays. The intricate oak pulpit took 15 years to carve and was completed in 1664.

Above: Fine arrangements of tall flowers flank the subtly-lit tomb of Admiral Michiel de Ruyter, the Dutch naval hero, in the choir of the Gothic Nieuwe Kerk

✝ **17 B2**

✉ **Nieuwe Kerk**
Dam Square

☎ 020 638 6909

🌐 **www.nieuwekerk.nl**

🕐 Daily 10–6 (also Sep–Oct, Thu 10–10); see website for more details

✋ Expensive

🚊 Tram: 4, 9, 14, 16, 24, 25

HRH Queen Beatrix's investiture in 1980, like those of her royal predecessors since 1815, took place in the Nieuwe Kerk. At this ceremony the new monarch takes an oath, and members of both chambers of Parliament swear allegiance to the throne. The national Remembrance Day service on 4 May takes place here each year and outside on Dam square. On 2 February 2002, the wedding between the Prince of Orange, Willem Alexander, and Princess Máxima took place here.

Oude Kerk

The original chapel on this site was built in the 13th century. By the 15th century it had been rebuilt in stone, but as the city grew the church became too small for its congregation. What is now known as Oude Kerk is the oldest building in Amsterdam.

Oude Kerk was the religious and social centre for much of Amsterdam, up until the late 16th century. It was open to all – people selling goods, beggars who needed a place to stay and the faithful. It became a Protestant Church during the Reformation.

The church was closed in 1951 after centuries of neglect and disrepair caused fear of its collapse. It took 28 years to complete the restoration. Inside, there are 15th- and 16th-century ceiling paintings, which had been covered with layers of blue paint in 1755 and remained hidden from view until 1955. Three restored stained-glass windows in the Lady Chapel depict the Death of the Virgin Mary. Another depicts the Treaty of Munster (1648). The lintel above the door to the red sacristy, where marriage licences were issued, bears the inscription "marry in haste, repent at leisure". The grave of Rembrandt's wife Saskia can also be seen in the church.

The Vater-Muller oak-encased organ, adorned with marbled-wood statues (1724), is renowned for its superb quality and summer concerts are held regularly.

Climb the tower, open at the weekend, for one of the best views of the city.

Above: Viewed from across a canal, the frequently extended frontage of Oude Kerk

✚ **17 C2**

✉ **Oude Kerk**
Oudekerksplein 23
Located on between
Warmoesstraat and
Oudezijds Voorburgwal

☎ 020 625 8284

🌐 **www.oudekerk.nl**

🕐 Mon–Sat 11–5, Sun 1–5;
closed 1 Jan,
30 Apr, 25 Dec

✋ Inexpensive

🚌 Tram: 4, 9, 16, 24, 25

Rembrandtplein

Rembrandtplein acquired its name in 1852 when the statue of the famous painter Rembrandt was unveiled on the square. It was Amsterdam's first statue. The square was previously called the Botermarkt, from its use as a butter market.

Rembrandt is also commemorated in the square by a group of large bronze statues depicting some of the figures in his most famous painting, *The Night Watch*, which is on display at the Rijksmuseum national gallery (see page 110).

Various hotels and cafés were built around the Rembrandtplein and it became a popular area for entertainment. Hotels from the 1800s include Schiller Karena and Café Schiller from 1892, De Kroon from 1898, a typical grand café, and Mille Colonnes from 1889. In the spring and summer the terraces are packed with people enjoying a drink, dining and people-watching and it is a main hangout for students and young locals. The patch of green grass in the centre provides the city's sun-worshippers with a place to lounge.

The square has also become a centre for Amsterdam nightlife. Large discos, nightclubs, gay clubs and numerous bars provide entertainment and music on and around the square. Given the crowd's exuberant behaviour, singing and carousing, at times this can be a fairly rowdy spot for out-of-towners.

There are several establishments dedicated to the gay community such as the joints on Reguliersdwarsstraat, via Halvemaansteeg, and along Amstel.

Reguliersdwarsstraat is also known for its hip clubs and upmarket restaurants. Close by are the Tuschinski Theatre, Willet-Holthuysen Museum, Kattenkabinet (Cat Cabinet) and the Tassenmuseum (Museum of Bags and Purses).

The art deco Tuschinski Theatre (see page 53) at Reguliersbreestraat 26–34 was built by Abraham Icek Tuschinski in 1921 as a cinema palace. During the 1940–1945 German occupation, the cinema was renamed "Tivoli", reverting to its original name after the war. Tuschinski and almost his entire family were murdered in the Nazi concentration camps.

Willet-Holthuysen Museum (see page 55) on Herengracht is the only fully furnished period patrician house on the canals that is open to the public.

Kattenkabinet (Herengracht 497; open: Tue–Fri 10–2, Sat–Sun 1–5; www. kattenkabinet.nl; admission: moderate) claims to be the only collection of objets d'art devoted solely to the theme of the cat.

At the Tassenmuseum (Herengracht 573; tel: 020 524 6452; www.tassenmuseum. nl; open daily 10–5; admission: moderate), you can admire an incredible assortment of styles, shapes and sizes of women's handbags collected by Hendrijke Ivo over a period of 30 years during her travels around Europe.

Left: A statue of Rembrandt keeps watch over Rembrandtplein

✚ **17 C4**

✉ **Rembrandtplein**

✋ Free

🚋 Tram: 4, 19, 14

🚆 51, 53, 54 Waterlooplein stop

Rosse Buurt/De Walletjes

Amsterdam's red light district is known as both the Rosse Buurt (red light neighbourhood) and De Walletjes (little walls). The area is criss-crossed by narrow alleyways, lined with seedy clubs, garish sex shops, neon-lit bars and peep shows. The red light district is one of the most popular tourist attractions in Amsterdam.

Visitors from all over the world wander through

✚ **17 C2**

✉ **Rosse Buurt/De Walletjes**
Red light district located in the area bordered by Zeedijk (north) Kloveniersburgwal (east) Damstraat (south) and Warmoesstraat (west)

🌐 **www.red-light-district.nl**

🚊 Tram: 1, 2, 4, 5, 9, 13, 16, 17, 24, 25

🚉 Centraal Station

these narrow streets. The scantily clad women sitting behind windows, hoping to attract customers, are accustomed to tourists. But do not try to take any pictures as photography is frowned upon here, and remember that this is also a residential area. The area is generally safe, but beware of pickpockets and drug addicts, and confine your sightseeing to daylight hours when tourists do not feel out of place.

Prostitution in Amsterdam dates back to the 13th century, and because of its port and sailor population, has long been an Amsterdam attraction.

By 1478 it had become so widespread that the city attempted to contain it. By the 1850s there were more than 200 brothels in the city.

The Dutch view is that prostitution cannot be stopped, but it can be controlled. Prostitutes are licensed, medically checked, and restricted to the red light areas. They even have their own trade union. The Prostitution Information Centre near Oude Kerk offers guided walking tours and there is a small gift shop (tel: 020 420 7328; www.pic-amsterdamcom).

Above: A house at Zeedijk

The Zeedijk

The Zeedijk was once part of the sea wall fortification of Amsterdam's early maritime settlement. It was built in the 1300s after Amsterdam had received its city charter. One of the remaining wood-fronted houses is located at No. 1, built in the 16th century as a sailors' hostel. The St Olofskapel, a seaman's church, lies opposite. By the 1600s, it had become a rat-infested, seedy area and remained run down until a clean-up campaign in the 1980s improved it considerably. Some good restaurants and bars were established on the Zeedijk, which is located on the fringe of the red light district. It is also home to some "alternative" museums on Oudezijds Achterburgwal.

Erotisch Museum

The Erotisch Museum contains five floors of erotica, a collection of erotic art from all over the world, and more, looking at the history of erotica over the centuries. Unique postcards, books and photographs are for sale. It has graphic adult content and is not for the faint-hearted.

Hash Marihuana Hemp Museum

The Hash Marihuana Hemp Museum traces the history of the cannabis plant and hashish. An "educational" tour informs you of the good things that ostensibly flow from assimilating hemp's multifarious by-products. You will see displays on historical, medicinal, recreational and practical uses of marihuana. The museum is next door to the Cannabis Connoisseurs' Club.

Venus Temple Sex Museum

The Venus Temple Sex Museum is the first museum of its kind which examines sex over the centuries through paintings, sculpture, etchings and photographs. This is the world's oldest sex museum and the exhibits here have been personally gathered by the owners. The displays are interesting and amusing and some of them are veritable antiques.

The Zeedijk

- ✉ **The Zeedijk**
- 🚊 Tram: 1, 2, 4, 5, 9, 13, 16, 17, 24, 25
- 🚉 Centraal Station

Erotisch Museum

- ✉ **Erotisch Museum**
  Oudezijds Achterburgwal 54
- ☎ 020 624 7303
- 🕐 Daily 11am–1am
- ✋ Moderate

Hash Marihuana Hemp Museum

- ✉ **Hash Marihuana Hemp Museum**
  Oudezijds Achterburgwal 148
- ☎ 020 623 5961
- 🌐 **www.hashmuseum.com**
- 🕐 Daily 10–10
- ✋ Moderate

Venus Temple Sex Museum

- ✉ **Venus Temple Sex Museum**
  Damrak 18
- ☎ 020 622 8376
- 🌐 **www.sexmuseumamsterdam.nl**
- 🕐 Daily 9:30am–11pm
- ✋ Inexpensive

Trippenhuis

The Trippenhuis is an architectural delight, and is actually two buildings, not one. The ornate Classical façade of the mansion is outlined by eight Corinthian columns, the central windows being false to preserve the symmetry. The two interiors are the mirror images of one another. The house was designed by Justus Vingboons for the brothers Louys and Hendrick Trip, who were wealthy arms merchants supplying most of Europe. The chimneys resemble cannons, a tribute to their family trade. The house, where they also conducted business negotiations, is conveniently located close to the Waag and Nieuwemarkt.

The emblem of a weapon and an olive branch in the stonework pertains to the metaphor "ex bello pax" – out of war comes peace. Ironically, the brothers were seen as peacemakers since they delivered the munitions needed to eventually bring about peace.

The Trippenhuis remained in the family until 1812 when Lodewijk Napoleon decided to set up the Royal Institute for Science, Literature and the Arts, the predecessor of the Royal Netherlands Academy of Arts and Sciences which currently occupies the building.

Across the street at No. 26 the Kleine Trippenhuis (small Trippenhuis) was built in 1698. The little building is only 2.5m (7 feet) wide and was once home to Mr Trip's coachman. The façade has two elaborately carved sphinxes. From 1817 to 1885 the city's art collection was housed here, after which it was moved to the then newly built Rijksmuseum.

Above: The Classical façade of the Trippenhuis

 17 C3

✉ **Trippenhuis**
Kloveniersburgwal 29

Closed to public

Tram: 4, 9, 16, 24, 25

Nieuwemarkt stop

Tuschinski Theatre

The Tuschinski Theatre is a remarkable building known for its wonderful potpourri of architectural styles. Art deco, art nouveau and the Amsterdam School all combined to create a richly decorated and rather fantastic interior. It is considered to be one of the most beautiful cinemas in the world.

The exterior has alligators guarding bronze doors, glazed tiles, ceramic sculptures and copper cupolas. Thousands of electric lamps, marble, stunning stained-glass windows and unique objets d'art enrich the interior. The theatre's exotic fairy-tale world features peacocks, cranes and butterflies.A hand-knotted oriental carpet, adds a colourful highlight in the otherwise sombre foyer with its dark wood carving and bronze decoration.

The lavish theatre was built in 1921 by the legendary Abram Icek Tuschinski (1886–1942), a Jewish émigré who fled the pogroms in Poland and came to the Netherlands. In Rotterdam he ran four cinemas and a hotel for emigrants who were about to sail for America. He moved to Amsterdam in 1917 with his two brothers-in-law, envisioning grand dreams of building a film palace. Tuschinski designed his theatre according to his own creative ideas and the artists he hired subsequently left their mark on this stunning building.

Neither Tuschinski nor his brothers-in-law survived World War II. A plaque to their memory hangs in the foyer. The theatre was completely restored in 2002 and is one of the most popular cinemas in Amsterdam. Guided tours are available in the summer. The illusionary world with its sumptuous interior is entertaining enough to be a film set in its own right.

Above: The fantastic foyer of the Tuschinski Theatre

⊞ 17 C4

✉ Pathé Tuschinski
Reguliersbreestraat 26–34

☎ 0900 1458 (Reservations)

W̅W̅W̅ www.tuschinski.nl

◔ Mon–Sun after 12:30pm

✋ See website for details

🚌 Tram: 4, 9, 16, 24, 25
Muntplein stop

Ⓜ Waterlooplein stop

Waag

The Waag is Amsterdam's oldest surviving gatehouse. The multi-turreted 1488 structure was once a main gate into the old city. It later became a weigh house and is now a restaurant, "In de Waag". It is sometimes referred to as St Antoniuspoort, its original name.

In former times prisoners condemned to public execution on the Nieuwemarkt would wait in the "little gallows room", and remnants of criminals were hung from the walls as a warning to others. The building became a public weigh house (*waaggebouw*) in 1617. Local farmers would have their produce weighed here for tax purposes and to make sure no one was cheated. Smugglers hoping to avoid taxes entered the city via the sewers underneath the Waag. Various guilds have occupied the upper rooms and at one time the Guild of Surgeons held its anatomy theatre here.

Nieuwemarkt, a paved open square on which the Waag stands, was a busy marketplace. The square is surrounded by an array of 17th- and 18th-century gabled houses. In the 1970s many houses were torn down in order to build the subway, sparking protests by conservationists which ultimately persuaded the city council to renovate rather than demolish. The Sunday antique market is held here from May to September.

If you follow St Antoniesbreestraat from Nieuwmarkt, you'll see the tall church tower of Zuiderkerk towards the Old Jewish Quarter. To the west of the market is the red light district and north is Chinatown with its oriental shops and restaurants.

Below: The Waag restaurant is a popular lunchtime venue

✚ **17 C2**

✉ **Waag**
Nieuwemarkt 4

☎ Restaurant 020 422 7772

🕐 Only the restauarant is open to the public

🚋 Tram: 9, 14

Ⓜ Nieuwemarkt

Willet-Holthuysen Museum

The Willet-Holthuysen Museum is a 17th-century patrician mansion with a lovely garden. The museum's period rooms give a glimpse into the lifestyle of the privileged merchant class in the 18th and 19th centuries. Highlights include furniture, silverware and a collection of paintings showcased in this well-preserved period house. The ornate gilded staircase is from 1740, and the 19th-century garden room overlooks the 18th-century intricate knot garden, laid out in French style. The Willet-Holthuysen families were fervent collectors of ceramics, glass and silver, and bequeathed their home and collection to the city of Amsterdam.

Above: A visitor finds something of interest in the Willet-Holthuysen Museum

Willet-Holthuysen Museum

✚ **17 C4**

✉ **Willet-Holthuysen Museum**
Herengracht 605

☎ 020 523 1822

🌐 **www.willetholthuysen.nl**

🕐 Mon–Fri 10–5, Sat–Sun 11–5; closed 1 Jan, 30 Apr and 25 Dec

✋ Inexpensive

🚋 Tram: 4, 9, 14 Rembrandtplein stop

Western Canals & Jordaan

Meandering along the Western Canals and through the bohemian Jordaan quarter provides visitors with a glimpse of some of Amsterdam's favourite sights – the Anne Frank House, thousands of houseboats along picturesque canals, art and antiques markets, stunning 17th- and 18th-century Dutch canal-house architecture, and quaint little "hofjes" or almshouses. Jordaan comes from the French *jardin* (garden), as many of the streets are named after flowers and trees. It is best known for its trendy shops, cafés and restaurants, and also includes three famous churches, the Palace of Justice, a theatre museum and another dedicated solely to tulips.

WESTERN CANALS & JORDAAN WALK

1. Westerkerk
See page 79

From Dam square, walk behind the Koninklijk Paleis, or Royal Palace (page 34) onto Raadhuisstraat. One street down to your right is Magna Plaza (page 38) shopping centre, converted from a former post office building. Continue along Raadhuisstraat to Westermarkt on the right, where you will find Westerkerk, with Rembrandt's unmarked grave.

2. Anne Frankhuis
See page 60

On Westermarkt is the Anne Frankhuis, once the hiding place of the brave Jewish girl whose diary is known worldwide. Also in view, three pink granite triangles by the water mark the Homomonument in remembrance of the gay men and women who were forced to wear this pink triangular symbol and who lost their lives in World War II.

3. Tulip Museum
See page 78

From the Anne Frankhuis, turn right along Prinsengracht until you reach Leiliegracht, and then turn left across the bridge to reach the Tulip Museum. Turn left and then right onto charming Bloemengracht, then take the second right into Tweede Leiliedwaarstraat. Continue to Egelantiersgracht (page 62), cross over the bridge and turn right.

4. Jordaan
See page 66

A left turn into Tweede Egelantiersdwarsboomstraat brings you into Jordaan, a typical Amsterdam district with brown cafés and unusual shops. Continue until you reach Westerstraat, turn right to the Pianola Museum (page 76). On Eersteboomdwarsstraat turn left to Lindengracht, then turn right and head for Brouwersgracht to look at the houseboats.

5. Herengracht
See page 63

Turn right down Prinsengracht to see Noorderkerk church. Return to Brouwersgracht and turn right following the street to the end. Turn right into Herengracht to see its lovely gabled houses. At Blauweburg bridge turn left, then right into Singel past the House with the Princes. At the Multatuli statue take Torensteeg and return to Dam square.

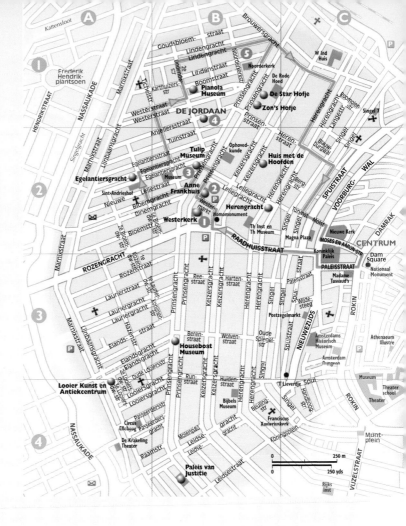

A Kattensloot

Frederik
Hendrik-
plantsoen

Goudsbloem- straat
Lindengracht
Lindengracht
Lindenstraat
Boomstraat
Pianola
Museum

Karthuizers-
str

Westerstraat
Westerstraat
Anjeliersstraat

DE JORDAAN

Tuinstraat

Egelantiersstraat
Egelantiersgracht
Egelantiersgracht
Egelantiersgracht

Egelantiersgracht
Museum

Tulip
Museum
Ophoved-
kunde
Huis met de
Hoofden

Sint-Andrieshof
Nieuwe

Leliestraat

Anne
Frankhuis

Leliestraat
Leliegracht

Bloemgracht
Dinemgracht
Bloemstr

Westerkerk

Herengracht
Homomonument

Marnixstraat

ROZENGRACHT

Rozengracht

RAADHUISSTRAAT

Laurierstraat
Lauriergracht
Lauriergracht

Reestraat
Hartenstraat

Prinsengracht
Keizersgracht
Keizersgracht

Herengracht
Herengracht
Singel

Lindbaansgracht

Elandsstraat
Elandsgracht
Elandsgracht

Hazenstr

Berenstraat
Houseboat
Museum

Wolvenstraat

Oude
Spiegelstr

Postzegelmarkt

Looier Kunst en
Antiekcentrum

Oude Loiersstr
Looiersgracht
Looiersgracht

Runstraat

Huidenstraat

Bijbels
Museum

Passeerdersstr
Passeerdersgracht

Circus
Elleboog
De Krakeling
Theater

Molenpad

Leidsegracht

Leidsestr

Raamstr

Paleis van
Justitie

NASSAUKADE

Brouwersgracht

W Ind
Huis

Noorderkerk

De Rode
Hoed

De Star Hofje

Zon's Hofje

Prinsenstraat

Herengracht
Singel 7

Keizersgracht

CENTRUM

Nieuwe Kerk

MOSES EN AARON-STR

Koninklijk
Paleis

PALEISSTRAAT

Madame
Tussaud's

Dam
Square
Nationaal
Monument

Wildesteeg

NIEUWEZIJDS

Amsterdams
Historisch
Museum

Amsterdam
Dungeon

Athenaeum
Illustre

Museum

Theater
school
Theater

ROKIN

Muntplein

VIJZELSTRAAT

'T Lieverdje

Beulingstr

Franciscus
Xaveriuskerk

Koningsplein

0   250 m
0   250 yds

Rijks
inst

Anne Frank Huis

The Anne Frank Stichting (foundation) was founded in 1957 to combat anti-Semitism and racism and to promote "the ideals set down in the diary of Anne Frank". Anne's greatest wish was to become a journalist and famous writer. Her diary was to serve as the basis for a book she hoped to publish entitled "the Secret Annexe".

During the Nazi German occupation of the Netherlands severe anti-Semitic measures were introduced. From 1942 until 1944 Anne Frank, her parents and sister, together with four other Jewish people, lived in hiding from the soldiers in the upper floors of this house, behind a moveable bookcase in a secret annexe. Anne described in detail and with great honesty her thoughts and feelings growing up under persecution. Her now famous diary records their daily life in confinement, their isolation and fear of discovery. Betrayal led to their discovery and all eight occupants were dispatched to concentration camps. Ironically, Anne Frank died a month before the war ended. Only Anne's father survived, and after the war he published his daughter's poignant words in 1947. *The Diary of Anne Frank* became an international best seller with millions of copies sold in more than 50 languages. It is one of the most-read books in the world.

Through restoration the building has been preserved much as it was when Anne and the others were arrested. Inside the house you can see the hinged bookcase separating the secret annexe from the rest of the building,

Anne's collection of photographs of royalty and filmstar postcards on the wall in the room where she slept, and the small gloomy rooms the families occupied. The visitor's centre has displays about Anne, and the millions of others who died in concentration camps.

Although not a large building, this is one of the most popular tourist attractions in Amsterdam, attracting almost a million visitors annually. It is best to go early to avoid the long queues.

Left: Visitors queuing outside Anne Frank's House; **below left:** A bronze bust of Anne Frank, set in front of the house where she and her family hid from the Nazis for more than two years

✚ **59 B2**

✉ **Anne Frank Huis**
Prinsengracht 267

☎ 020 556 7100

🔤 **www.annefrank.org**

🕐 15 Mar–14 Sep, daily 9–9; 15 Sep–14 Mar, 9–7; closed Yom Kippur

💷 Moderate

🚌 21, 170, 171, 172 Westermarkt stop Museumboat stop 7; Tram: 13, 17

Egelantiersgracht

This lovely little canal retains much of its original character despite some city development. The canals in this area were named after trees and flowers; the name Egelantiersgracht is from the flowering eglantine rose, or sweet briar.

The houses in this area were built for artisans. They are smaller, more intimate and not as grand as the mansions along the main canals Prinsengracht, Keizersgracht and Herengracht. There is huge demand for canalside houses in Jordaan. One of the loveliest spots along the

canal is St Andrieshofje at Egelantiersgracht 107–114. The hofje with its 36 houses was built in 1617 and remodelled in 1884. The passageway is lined with beautiful blue and white Delft tiles and leads to a small courtyard with a lovely garden. An old water pump with a stone inscription "Vrede Sy Met U" (Peace Be With You) stands here. At Nos 61–65, a carved stone falcon adorns the gable stone of the three simple bell-gabled houses.

In the summer the bridges are lined with flowerboxes adding a splash of colour to this idyllic canal. The atmosphere is one of

tranquillity and rest. Canal-side cafés are popular and can often be found on the canal corners. The carillon bells of Westerkerk can be heard chiming regularly. It is said that all true Jordaaners are born within hearing distance of the bells.

The hardware store at Nos 2–6 with its wrought-iron ornaments and intricate brickwork is a fine example of the distinctive Amsterdam School of architecture, and dates from 1917.

Above: A passenger alights at the Egelantiersgracht café, a haunt of artists on the banks of Prinsengracht

59 A2

✉ **Egalantiersgracht**
Between Lijnbaansgracht and Prinsengracht

✋ Free

🚌 Tram: 13, 14, 17

Herengracht

There is no better place to experience Golden Age Amsterdam than Herengracht. It was one of the most attractive and elegant districts of its time, and still is today, where 17th-century merchants' houses line the canal banks.

Herengracht is one of three canals (the other two being Keizersgracht and Prinsengracht) built in concentric rings to accommodate four lanes of medium-sized ships that would moor and unload cargo directly in front of the merchants' houses. This model has been much studied and admired by the city planners of other countries around the world.

Built between 1612 and 1658 on a design drawn up by municipal carpenter, Hendrick Staets, the Herengracht is 3.5km (2.2 miles) long, Keizersgracht 4km (2.5 miles) and Prinsengracht 4.5km (2.8 miles). During the second half of 17th century, the Herengracht was the most sought after residential district. It was so popular that the magistrate had to confine the width of the aristocrats' houses to 8m (26 feet). Today, no fewer than 400 houses are protected monuments.

The "Gouden Bocht" (Golden Arc) of the Herengracht, comprising houses numbered 464–436 (between Vijzelstraat and Leidestraat) is especially noteworthy for its magnificently decorated structures. Number 527 Herengracht, built in 1667, has an interesting history: Tsar Peter the Great of Russia lived here during a visit to the Netherlands. Today, the houses are mostly occupied by banks and offices or are used as museum buildings; they have become too large and too expensive to be used as dwellings.

Above: Fine houses of 17th-century merchants and aristocrats line the banks of Herengracht

✚ **59 B2**

✉ **Herengracht**

🚊 Tram: 1, 2, 4, 5, 13, 14, 16, 17, 24, 25

🚤 Museumboat stop: 4, 7

Houseboat Museum

More than 2,500 houseboats line the canals of Amsterdam, many sprouting delightful little gardens. These floating homes appeal to people who prefer an alternative lifestyle living afloat. At the Houseboat Museum you can climb onboard and see for yourself.

Also known in Dutch as Woonbootmuseum, the 1914 river barge Hendrika Maria

✚ **59 B3**

✉ **Houseboat Museum**
Prinsengracht opposite No 296

☎ 020 427 0750

🌐 **www.houseboat museum.nl**

🕐 Mar–Oct, Tue–Sun 11–5; Nov–Feb, Fri–Sun 11–5; closed 1 Jan, 30 Apr, 25–26, 31 Dec

✋ Inexpensive

🚌 Tram: 1, 2, 5, 7, 10, 13, 14, 17

once carried sand, gravel and coal until the 1960s when it was converted into a cosy houseboat. No one lives onboard today, but you are welcome to make yourself at home in the comfortable armchairs. Coffee is served in the surprisingly spacious living room and folk are on hand to answer your questions.

The housing crisis after World War II increased the number of houseboat dwellers substantially.

The museum has information about houseboat living and although many dream of it, the reality is that houseboats require a large amount of care and maintenance. A slide show makes this clear. Every three to four years the boat

must be taken out of the water and cleaned with a high pressure hose to remove barnacles and other corrosive accretions, loose bolts are replaced and on occasion sections of the hull if they have become thin. All registered boats have postal addresses and are connected to city electricity mains. In days gone by, the Prinsengracht, lined with merchants' homes and warehouses, was an important thoroughfare where cargo would be unloaded from ships by means of massive hoist-beams seen in the gables of many buildings.

Above: Exterior view of the Houseboat Museum

Huis met de Hoofden

There are many splendid decorations on the façades of the old houses of Amsterdam, and this one is no exception. The Huis met de Hoofden was built in 1622 and is one of the largest double houses in Dutch Renaissance style.

This step-gable house is known as the House with the Heads, so named because of the façade with six heads placed upon pilasters. Legend has it that they commemorate a brave housemaid armed with an axe who surprised seven burglars and cut off the heads of the first six, but fell in love with the seventh and married him instead. The sculptures, in fact, portray the six classical deities (from left to right): Apollo, Ceres, Mars, Minerva, Bacchus and Diana. The façade is attributed to Pieter de Keyser, the son of architect Hendrick Keyser. The building houses the Bureau Monumenten en Archeologie, (BMA), a foundation which supervises the care and protection of Amsterdam's officially recognised public monuments and archaeological finds. In 2007 BMA will move to De Bazel building on Vijzelstraat 32 and the J R Ritman library, Bibliotheca Philosophica Hermetica, a scholarly yet publicly accessible library specialising in Christian-Hermetic spirituality, will be housed here eventually in the House with the Heads.

At Keizersgracht 209 is a 1734 house featuring a female statue symbolising hope. Number 319 was built by Philips Vingeboons in 1639 and has an unusual highly decorated façade embellished with scrolls, garlands and vases. At No 323 a Louis XIV house from 1728 has a raised cornice and two hoisting beams, and three graceful neck gables at Nos 353–57 are from the early 18th century.

Above: Four of the heads on the Huis met de Hoofden

✚ **59 B2**

✉ **Huis met de Hoofden**
Keizersgracht 123

🕐 Closed for refurbishment until Bibliotheca Philosophica Hermetica moves in

🚋 Tram: 13, 14, 17

Jordaan

In Amsterdam the farther away one lived from the Herengracht, the less prestigious the address. The Jordaan quarter was laid out in the marshy areas beyond the fashionable canals and this is where workers whose industries were banned from the city centre set up shop. It was also home to immigrants fleeing religious persecution, such as the French Huguenots.

The Jordaan was the most crowded part of the city, and by the early days of the 20th century its tightly knit streets and canals had become a rundown slum. Massive redevelopment plans were drawn up in the 1970s to tear everything down and build modern housing. Protests followed, and fortunately the decision was made to restore the buildings that could be saved, and preserve the essential character of the neighbourhood.

Today, the Jordaan is known as a somewhat fashionable and slightly bohemian place to live, and for its abundance of interesting and quirky small shops, and cafés. Visitors enjoy exploring the side streets, picturesque narrow canals, trendy boutiques and unusual almshouses known as hofjes.

Bruin (brown) cafés are typically Dutch; the name comes from their brown, tobacco smoke-stained wooden interiors. Liquor,

coffee and snacks are served. You'll find them everywhere in the Jordaan, but two examples are t' Smaaltje, (Egelantiersgracht 12), and De Pieper (Prinsengracht 424), a 300-year-old bruin café complete with sand on the floor and a beamed ceiling.

Above: A stunning roof-garden adorns a canal houseboat in the Jordaan district

☩ **59 B1**

✉ **Jordaan**
Boundaries are Brouwersgracht (north), Leidsegracht (south), Singelgracht (east), Prinsengracht (west)

🖐 Free

🚌 Tram: 13, 14, 17

Jordaan Hofjes

A very Dutch characteristic of the Jordaan is its hofjes, or almshouses. By bequeathing money for a home for the needy in the 17th century, some wealthy Dutchmen would "buy their way into heaven". Hofjes consist of small houses built around an interior courtyard garden, protected behind a port door.

Hofjes are quiet, often isolated places, and quite lovely. Before the "Alteration" to Protestantism, the Catholic Church provided subsidised housing for the poor and elderly in need, mostly widows. Many of these former hospices are occupied nowadays by senior citizens and the peace and tranquillity of hofje living is evident within. You are welcome to visit the courtyards of most hofjes, as long as you respect the peace and quiet of the surroundings and the privacy of those living there.

The Claes Claesz Anslohofje (1626), the "house with the writing hand", is on Eerste Egelantiersdwarsstraat and has three inner courtyards. It is now a hall of residence for music students. Enter through the wooden door across the street from No. 4. Above the entrance to a restaurant is a tablet bearing the coat of arms of "Anslo", a former Dutch name for Oslo. Four other hofjes in the Jordaan are the Hofje Venetiae (1670), Elandsstraat 102–142; Hofje Pieter – Jansz Suyckerhoff (1667) Lindengracht 149–163;

the Broenshofje at Boomstraat 52; and the Karthuizerhof 89–171 Kaarthuizerstraat, now home to a younger group. You will find that many of the houses in the Jordaan have interesting gable stones on the front façades of the buildings. Some of these carved stones indicated the trade of the owners, such as a tobacconist at Prinsengracht 226, or a butcher at Tweede Goudsbloemdwarsstraat 26.

Above: A hofje in Karlhuizerstraat in the Jordaan district overlooks a peaceful courtyard

⊞ 59 B1

⊠ Jordaan Hofjes

🚋 Tram: 13, 14, 17

Looier Kunst en Antiekcentrum

The Looier Kunst en Antiekcentrum was established here 30 years ago and is the largest permanent indoor antique market in the Netherlands. In the 17th century the main industry was tanning, so the area is also known as Tanners Canal.

Located near the Leidseplein, De Looier can easily be reached from there by tram or on foot. It is extensive and is one of the few covered markets in Amsterdam. Because of this, it's a great place to visit if the weather is inclement or you feel like shopping in a market that is considered by many to be a collectors' paradise.

Left and above: Items displayed at the Looier Kunst en Antiekcentrum

⊞ **59 A4**

✉ **Looier Kunst en Antiekcentrum**
Elandsgracht 109

☎ 020 624 9038

🖳 **www.looier.nl**

🕐 Sat–Thu 11–5

✋ Free

🚌 Tram: 7, 10, 17 Elandsgracht stop

The antique and art market has 72 stalls, around 90 showcases, several larger shops and a delightful café, Brasserie Brasz. On Wednesdays and on the weekends there is a flea market as well on the market square, where all types of people rent space and sell pieces of art, antiques, curios and other bric-a-brac.

Other items for sale in De Looier include a diverse selection of glassware, porcelain, ceramics (including Delft Blue), jewellery, gold, silver, furniture, paintings, prints, mirrors, clocks, coins, costumes, ornaments, Bakelite, pewter, enamel, dolls, tin plate toys, pens, Asian and religious art and much more.

Unlike many antique markets De Looier booths do not have people manning them. Instead you need to note down the number of the booth and then approach the nearest service bell to ring for assistance. A salesperson will quickly come over to help you. It is possible to bargain if you know the value of the item you wish to buy.

If you work up a hunger or thirst shopping and browsing, the café in De Looier provides light snacks and refreshments for visitors apart from providing a pleasant environment to unwind in.

Specialised collectors search for finds in the market and some pieces have even ended up in museums. In fact, many of the *antiquairs* located here deal only with museums or well-known collectors. It is a fun place to browse – you never know what treasures you may come across.

Left: A colourful display of antiques and other bric-a-brac at the Looier Kunst en Antiekcentrum

Paleis van Justitie

City architect Jan de Greef converted the former city orphanage, Almoezeniersweeshuis, into the imposing Palace of Justice with its neoclassical façade, Corinthian pilasters and balustrades along the roofline in the early 19th century.

The orphanage opened in 1663 with space for 800 children. More than 2,000 homeless youngsters were crowded into the building by 1811. A royal decree was passed permitting the orphans to be relocated to other towns. By the time this act was implemented in 1822, there were widespread protests from alarmed Amsterdammers who accused the authorities of stealing the children. When all of the children had been relocated the orphanage was closed.

The conversion of the building was completed in 1829. The courtrooms inside are on either side of two open yards. The second floor housed the Stadsbibliotheek city library from 1838 to 1863 and the left wing served as an emergency hospital from 1833 to 1875. Over the years, a shortage of office space necessitated numerous interior renovations, including the construction of workspace in the interior courtyards. In 1950, the city of Amsterdam purchased properties lying next to and behind the Paleis van Justitie on Prinsengracht, Leidsegracht and Lange Leidsedwarsstraat providing additional space for expansion.

In 1990 many of the numerous judicial services moved to a new complex on the Parnassusweg. The building today houses the Amsterdam Court of Appeal.

The Prinsengracht is the third canal in the "Grachtengordel" (Canal Girdle) dug out during the Golden Age and is a favourite canal for visitors to walk along.

Left: A barge moored by a bridge spanning the Prinsengracht canal; **above:** Trees framing tall, narrow houses bordering Prinsengracht

✚ **59 B4**

✉ **Paleis van Justitie**
Prinsengracht 434–436

☎ 020 541 2111

🕐 Mon–Fri 9–5

♿ Free, with restrictions

🚋 Tram: 1, 2, 5, 6, 7, 10

Pianola Museum

Automatic pianos were introduced in 1900 and became a musical rage. Fifteen instruments and related objects are showcased here along with nearly 20,000 pianola rolls, all carefully preserved, in the museum's archive. Nearly all of them can be played on the different instruments in the museum.

The player piano could be played automatically by means of a pneumatic mechanism, or by hand. Hand controls and foot-pedals enabled the player to influence the tempo, and expression, and make a musical rendering of a particular piece. Perforated paper music rolls were used to produce a wide variety of music.

The reproducing piano was the fully automatic version of the player piano. These instruments will play back the performance of a pianist which has been recorded on a music roll. Special equipment connected to the pianist's keyboard in the studio of the roll-factory produced the master rolls. Composers such as Ravel, Strauss, Debussy and Mahler all recorded pieces for use in the reproducing piano in this manner.

The player piano industry was successful for around 30 years. The majority of the rolls produced were of the 88-note type, which became the world standard in 1910. A reproducing piano can play only the rolls recorded for the instrument itself.

With the exception of July and August, monthly concerts are held in the museum, in which different aspects of the pianola music are presented.

Below: The entrance to the Pianola Museum

 59 B1

⊠ **Pianola Museum**
Westerstraat 106

☎ 020 627 9624

www.pianola.nl

Sun 11:30–5; group tours all week by appointment

18 Marnixbad stop; Tram: Tram 3, 10, 13, 14, 17

Star Hofje & Zon's Hofje

Within a short walk of each other on lovely Prinsengracht are two of the area's most charming hofjes. There are some 200 hofjes in the Netherlands of which Amsterdam can boast 47 of its original 51, and half of these are located in the Jordaan where land was cheap.

Hofjes are built behind the street buildings usually in a square or U-shaped layout with a courtyard in the middle. The first hofjes were built in the Jordaan and a number of them still serve their original purpose of social housing.

The lovely Star Hofje was built on the site of the former Star brewery in 1804. It is officially known as the Van Breinen hofje, named after the man who founded the almshouse. According to legend, Jacob van Breinen was accidentally locked in a vault, and he was so grateful for his release that he built the hofje.

The tranquil courtyard garden has a large laburnum tree offering shade to the flowering garden and benches where residents and visitors may rest.

The Zon's Hofje is built on the side of the De Zon clandestine Mennonite church and meetings were held in the courtyard named Kleine Zon or Little Sun, hence the name of the hofje. In 1720 the name was changed to De Arke Noach (Noah's Ark). The church was demolished in 1755 and is commemorated by a plaque in the courtyard. A lintel above Nos 161–163 from the former church shows animals going in pairs into Noah's Ark.

Above: The entrance of the Star Hofje, one of Prisengracht's most interesting hofjes

De Star Hofje

✚ 59 B1

✉ **De Star Hofje**
Prinsengracht 89–133

🕒 Mon–Fri 6–6, Sat 6–2

🚊 Tram: 3, 10, 13, 14, 17

Zon's Hofje

✚ 59 B1

✉ **Zon's Hofje**
Prinsengracht 159–171

🕒 Mon–Fri 10–5

🚊 Tram: 3, 10, 13, 14, 17

Tulip Museum

The Tulip Museum is filled with just about anything you ever wanted to know, see or smell about this ubiquitous, typically Dutch flower. Actually, the tulip's origin is in Turkey. Before the Dutch became tulip fanatics, the Sultans of the Ottoman Empire cultivated this beautiful flower in their lavish palaces, and maintained blissful gardens filled with stunning, vibrant blooms.

In the 17th century the most prized tulips were the multi-coloured "broken" tulips of white or gold, streaked with vibrant flames of bright violet, red or brown. The glorious mutations of colour were caused by a virus. Fortunes were bid for bulbs during this period known as "Tulipomania" – a year's salary was offered for just one bulb. When the market became saturated, prices fell and many fortunes were lost.

In the Bloemenbollenwinkel musem shop, a wide variety of bulbs can be purchased in specific seasons and shipped worldwide, accompanied by international health certificates. Tulips in many varieties and colours, daffodils, hyacinths, amaryllis, paper whites, crocus, dahlias and more are on sale. A large collection of antique tiles, cards, posters, purses, pillows and other household items with tulip motifs make a popular gift or souvenir from a visit to Amsterdam. Books about the history of the tulip, its cultivation and the joy of flowering bulbs are always available.

✚ **59 B2**

✉ **Tulip Museum**
Prinsengracht 112

☎ 020 421 0095

▨ **www.amsterdam
tulipmuseum.com**

◷ Tue–Sun 10–6

🚌 21, 170, 171, 172
Westerkerk stop;
Tram: 13, 17

Above: Detail of a yellow and red streaked tulip growing at the Keukenhof Gardens

Westerkerk

Of the four churches built in the 17th century to the north, south, east and west of the centre of Amsterdam, the Westerkerk is by far the most beautiful. The 85m (280 feet) tower is the tallest in the city and the spectacular panoramic view from the top makes the climb worthwhile.

The church has the largest nave and the largest congregation as well as the tallest tower commonly called "Lange Jan" (Tall John). The golden crown atop is a symbol of the city granted by the Hapsburg Emperor Maxmillian 150 years earlier. Westerkerk is the masterwork of Hendrick de Keyser who died in 1621, one year after construction began. It was completed ten years later by his son Pieter with Cornelis Dancker. The carillon chimes automatically every 15 minutes, but its 50 bells are played by hand every Thursday from noon to 1pm. Rembrandt was buried in the church in 1669, but the location is not known. His son Titus is buried here as well. The church is laid out in the form of a double Greek cross. Its whitewashed interior contains a massive organ adorned with musical instruments and frescoes by Gerard de Lairesse, a student of Rembrandt.

Outside on the Westermarkt square is the Homomonument of three granite triangles, in remembrance of the gay men and lesbian women who lost their lives in World War II (www.homomonument.nl). The Westerkerk is almost next door to the Anne Frank House. Visitors often lay flowers at the foot of the statue of Anne Frank located outside the church. When she was in hiding she used to listen to the church carillon before the bells were melted down by the Nazis.

Left: The church and imposing tower of Westerkerk

✚ **59 B2**

✉ **Westerkerk**
Prinsengracht 281

☎ 020 624 7766

🌐 **www.westerkerk.nl**

🕐 Apr–Sep, Mon–Fri 11–3; Tower climb Apr–Sep, Mon–Sat every hour; Oct–Mar call 020 689 2565

✋ Church free; Tower inexpensive

🚋 Tram: 13, 14, 17

🚤 Museumboat: Stop 7

Eastern Canals

The Jewish Quarter of Amsterdam was located in the Eastern Canals area. Amsterdam was home to 80,000 of the country's pre-war Jewish community and most lived in this section of town. It was a colourful area, its centre the busy Waterlooplein market, the shopping street Jodenbreestraat, and the complex of synagogues that now make up the Joods Historisch Museum, which together with the the Verzetsmuseum of the Dutch resistance, all bear witness to a poignant history. Artis Zoo, Hortus Botanicus botanical gardens and the Tropenmuseum provide a look at the flora and fauna from near and far, while three churches – Amstelkerk, Zuiderkerk and Mozes en Aäronkerk are faithful reminders of the city's Christian tradition.

EASTERN CANALS WALK

1. Zuiderkerk
See page 97
Start at the 15th-century Waag (page 54), Amsterdam's oldest surviving gatehouse which also served as a public weigh house. On the Nieuwemarkt, take St Antonius Breestraat to 17th-century Zuiderkerk, a prominent landmark with its impressive steeple and onion dome.

2. Rembrandthuis
See page 92
Continue straight ahead to Jodenbreestraat and the Rembrandhuis, once home to one of the Netherlands' most famous painters. At the end of the street is Mr Visserplein with the imposing twin-towered Mozes en Aäronkerk (page 96). In front of the church is Waterlooplein, famous for its outdoor market (page 96).

3. Joods Historisch Museum
See page 88
From Waterlooplein take Weesperstraat to the Joods Historisch Museum for a fascinating look at Jewish history. Across the street is the Portuguese Israëlitische Synagogue (page 91). In front on Daniel Meyerplein is a statue of "the Dockworker", commemorating the February strike against the deportation of Jews during World War II.

4. Hermitage Museum
See page 33
Crossing over Nieuwe Herengracht, you will find the Hermitage Museum, showing collections on loan from the St Petersburg museum in Russia. Turn right to continue to the Amstel river where the famous Magere Brug (page 37) spans the water. Return via Nieuwe Keizersgracht to Plantage Parklaan to visit the botanical gardens.

5. Hortus Botanicus & Artis Zoo
See pages 86 & 84
Hortus Botanicus botanical gardens and Wertheim Park are on the left. Turning right into Plantage Middenlaan will take you to the Hollandse Schouwburg, a deportation centre in World War II. Down the road on the left is Artis Zoo. Reaching Mauritskade you will see the Tropenmuseum and Tropentheatre (page 93) straight ahead, with Oosterpark behind.

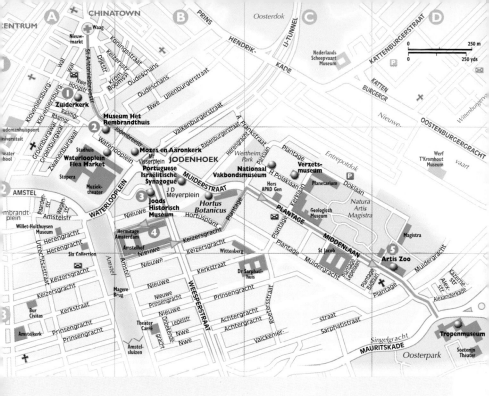

Artis Zoo

The name Artis comes from the Latin "Artis Natura Magistra" (Nature, Mistress of the Arts). There is a strong focus on education in the five elements that make up Artis: Zoo and Aquarium, Botanical Gardens, Zoological Museum, Geological Museum and Planetarium.

Established in 1838, Artis Zoo is the oldest in continental Europe. Covering 14ha (34 acres), with its winding paths, 200 types of trees, ponds and formal gardens, it still retains a 19th-century atmosphere. There are more than 700 species of animals living in Artis, some 6,100 creatures, a house for nocturnal animals, a beautiful hippo house and an authentic African savannah enclosure. There is also a spacious aviary, and a Children's Farm, European bison, birds of prey, amphibians, reptiles, insects – on the whole a magnificent overview of the entire animal kingdom!

Zoo admission also gives access to the two museums in the park and the Aquarium. The Geological Museum has a wealth of fossils, minerals and interesting geological models showing the development of the earth. The Aquarium with its colourful marine life is the largest in the Netherlands.

Artis Planetarium gives you an opportunity to stargaze. Watch the moon passing through its various phases as day changes to night before your eyes.

The enormous projector is a technical marvel consisting of more than 29,000 separate elements.

Left: Enjoying the sunshine outside the large dome of the Planetarium; **above:** The Artis logo depicts its five elements

- **83 D3**
- ✉ **Artis Zoo**
  Plantage Kerklaan 38–40
- ☎ 020 523 3400
- 🌐 www.artis.nl
- 🕐 Daily 9–5 (also summer 9–6); Planetarium closed Mon 9–12:30
- ✋ Expensive (also includes Aquarium, museums and Planetarium)
- 🚋 Tram: 9, 10, 14 Waterlooplein stop
- ❓ Dogs not allowed in Zoo

Hortus Botanicus Amsterdam

Near Artis Zoo, Hortus Botanicus is a wonderful botanical gardens founded in 1682, and one of the oldest of its kind in the world. It now boasts more than 6,000 plants (some 4,000 species) from around the planet, growing in its gardens and greenhouses.

Originally, the Hortus was a medicinal herb garden, founded in 1638 by the Amsterdam City Council. Herbs were of vital importance as the basis of medicines. Doctors and pharmacists were trained in the preparation of medicinal prescriptions at the Hortus.

Ships from the Dutch East India Company returned from their voyages bearing new species of plants and the Hortus rapidly expanded in the 17th and 18th centuries. Along with herbs and spices, the ships also brought exotic ornamental plants. The 300-year-old Eastern Cape giant cycad in the Palm House dates from that period.

Treats in store inside this oasis of tranquillity are many and varied. The Mexican/Californian Desert House features plants native to that part of the American continent. There is a nursery nurturing exotic orchids, and a butterfly house filled with hundreds of butterflies and plants. The Palm House contains the largest, oldest and rarest plants, while the Three Climates Greenhouse has tropical, sub-tropical and desert dry climates all in one.

You will find one of the most beautiful outdoor cafés in Amsterdam, The Orangery, in the middle of the gardens.

Above: Inside the Three Climates Greenhouse; **left:** You can enjoy outdoor gardens and indoor greenhouses at Hortus Botanicus

✚ **83 B2**

✉ **Hortus Botanicus Amsterdam**
Plantage Middenlaan 2a

☎ 020 625 9021

📶 **www.hortus-botanicus.nl**

🕐 Mon–Fri 9–5, Sat–Sun 10–5 (also summer 9–9; Dec–Jan, Mon–Fri 9–4); closed 1 Jan, 25 Dec

✋ Moderate

🚋 Tram: 9, 14 Mr Visserplein stop

🚇 51, 53, 54 Waterlooplein stop

🚢 Museum boat: Stop 3

Joods Historisch Museum

Four Ashkenazi synagogues built between 1671 and 1752, and among the finest buildings in the city, house the Joods Historisch Museum. The exhibitions are devoted to Judaism and present the history, culture and religion of the Jewish community in Amsterdam.

This is the largest and most important Jewish museum outside Israel. After World War II the buildings lay in ruins for decades. The massive complex in the heart of the former Jewish neighbourhood was reconstructed at a cost of 6 million and opened in 1987. The synagogues are connected by interior walkways.

In 1930, the original Jewish Historical Museum was founded to illustrate Jewish life and encourage Jewish studies. Most of the collection was confiscated during the war. Of the 610 pieces, only 140 were recovered by the museum. Today, thanks to many contributions, there are more than 11,000 works of art, ceremonial items and historical objects, around 5 per cent of which are on permanent display. Special exhibitions are presented and the museum also has exhibits out on loan. The museum's Resource Centre has more than 43,000 books, brochures, documents, photos, audio and video material; a good deal of the museum collection may also be accessed via the website.

The Great Synagogue (1671) documents the Jewish community's contribution in trade and industry to the city's economic life before the war. In the New Synagogue (1752) there are displays of religious objects and a detailed history of Zionism. The Holy Ark (1791) and the Haggadah Manuscript (1734) are the highlights, as well as a Festival Prayer Book from 1669, one of the few to survive the Middle Ages. The displays also tell the chilling story of the Holocaust. The Dutch Jewish community was decimated, 102,000 people were exterminated. The museum also has a children's exhibition and special events for them. The museum is a monument to the strength and enduring faith of the Jewish people as well as a memorial to their suffering under the Nazis.

Left: A Star of David marks the entrance to the Joods Historisch Museum

✚ **83 B2**

✉ **Joods Historisch Museum**
Nieuwe Amstelstraat 3–5

☎ 020 531 0310

🌐 **www.jhm.nl**

🕐 Daily 11–5 (also Thu 11–9); closed Jewish hols

✋ Moderate

🚋 Tram: 9, 14

🚇 51, 53, 54 Waterlooplein stop

⛴ Museum boat: Stop 3

Mozes en Aäronkerk

The official Roman Catholic name of Mozes en Aäronkerk is Saint Anthony of Padua (Sint Antoniuskerk), who was one of the first followers of St Francis of Assisi (1181–1224). The Mozes en Aäronkerk was established in 1641 as a hidden church.

In 1304 the first Franciscan friars settled in Amsterdam. In 1578 a group of leading Protestant businessmen overthrew the Catholic government, declaring the city Protestant, even though 95 per cent of the population was Catholic. Worship in public was officially forbidden for Catholics, so in 1641 some leading Catholics purchased a house in Breestraat (now called Jodenbreestraat) where a small statue of Moses stood. A Franciscan priest began to celebrate

Mass there in secret, and in 1691 when the parish had secured additional houses around "Moses", including the adjacent house with its statue of Aäron, a much larger church was built near Waterlooplein and the church acquired its nickname of "Moses and Aäron Church".

The present church dates from 1841 and is built on the site of the 17th-century secret church. The organ is from 1871. The middle section of the High Altar is from the original baroque

church. The stone statues of Moses and Aäron can still be seen outside near the rear wall of the church.

In 1969 it ceased to be used as a parish church. There are, however, many activities that take place regularly in the building, in particular at Mozeshuis next door – an adult education centre. It is also used for exhibitions, concerts, symposia and meetings.

Below: The ornate towers above the 19th-century neoclassical façade of Mozes en Aäronkerk

✚ **83 B2**

✉ **Mozes en Aäronkerk**
Waterlooplein 205

☎ 020 622 1305

🌐 **www.mozeshuis.nl**

✷ Events only

🚊 Tram: 9, 14

🚌 51, 53, 54 Waterlooplein
stop

⛴ Museum boat:
Muziektheater

Portuguese Israëlitische Synagogue

When it was built in 1675 this was the largest synagogue in the world, and one of the first of any size to be built in Western Europe. It is still largely in its original state. The design by Elias Bouwman was inspired by the impressive Temple of Solomon in Jerusalem.

The Portuguese Israëlitische Synagogue was built for Amsterdam's Portuguese Sephardic community. In 1492 Spain expelled its Jewish population and many went to Portugal. After the Inquisition, they came to Amsterdam. The Netherlands and Spain were at war, so the community called itself "Portuguese Jews", not to be confused with the enemy. In 1597 the first member of the Jewish community was granted Dutch citizenship. Judaism has been practised openly in the city since 1602.

The enormous building has a rectangular floor plan. The layout is of the longitudinal Iberian-Sephardic type with the Hechal (Holy Ark) in the southeast corner

facing towards Jerusalem and the tebah (bimah) at the opposite end of the interior. The seating is divided into two equal halves facing one another and separated by an aisle. The deal floor is covered with fine sand, in the old Dutch fashion, to absorb dust, moisture and dirt from shoes and to muffle the noise.

The wooden ceiling is barrel-vaulted with four Ionic columns supporting it. There are 72 windows and the interior is illuminated by more than 1,000 candles. It is remarkable that the building escaped destruction during World War II; it was left untouched. The library here is one of the oldest Jewish libraries in Europe.

Above: The Portuguese Synagogue, one of the largest synagogues in Europe

✚ **83 B2**

✉ **Portuguese Israëlitische Synagogue**
Mr L E Visserplein 3

☎ 020 624 5351

🌐 **www.esnoga.com**

🕐 Apr–Oct, Sun–Fri 10–4; Nov–Mar, Sun–Thu 10–4, Fri 10–2, Sat service 9am; closed Jewish hols

💷 Expensive

🚊 Tram: 9, 14

🚌 51, 53, 54 Waterlooplein stop

Rembrandthuis

Artist Rembrandt van Rijn lived here from 1639 to 1660. The house built in 1606 exhibits 250 of his 300 etchings. Some of the most productive years of his life, and the saddest, were spent here.

The house has been restored to look as it did when Rembrandt lived here, complete with furnishings,

➕ **83 A2**

✉️ **Rembrandthuis**
Jodenbreestraat 4

☎️ 020 520 0400

🌐 **www.rembrandthuis.nl**

🕐 Daily 10–5

✋ Expensive

🚌 Tram: 9, 14 Waterlooplein stop

Ⓜ️ 51, 53, 54 Waterlooplein stop

artwork and objects taken from Rembrandt's original inventory drawn up when he was forced to sell the house in 1656. On show are some of the art and curios he amassed in his lifetime, as well as his large painting studio, the smaller printing room for his etchings, his cabinet of plaster models and various decorative items, and paintings by his teacher Pieter Lastman and works by Rembrandt's apprentices.

Born in Leiden in 1609, Rembrandt had become a well-known artist by the time he moved to Amsterdam in 1631. He later married Saskia van Uylenburgh, but sadly their three children didn't survive. Saskia also

died shortly after the birth of their son Titus, a sickly child who died young. Rembrandt received significant commissions in the prosperous city of Amsterdam and some of his most famous works were painted in this house, including *The Night Watch*. His students also came to the house to study and work with him in a studio on the top floor. As the years passed, his extravagant lifestyle forced him into bankruptcy and he died in an apartment in the Jordaan. His famous paintings and drawings may also be admired in the Rijksmuseum.

Above: Entrance to the Rembrandhuis museum

Tropenmuseum

The Tropenmuseum is part of the Royal Tropical Institute (KIT), a knowledge institute for international and inter-cultural collaboration and the largest anthropological museum in the country. Focusing on "one world, a thousand stories", the displays in life-like settings take you around the globe – inside a Javanese courtyard, a Bombay slum, a Nigerian bar, or a noisy Arab street and a Hindu temple.

As one of Europe's leading ethnographic museums, and renowned for its exhibits, it was originally established in 1859 as a collection of objects from the Dutch colonies "for the instruction and amusement of the Dutch people".

In the 1920s the Colonial Institute, decorated with stone friezes commemorating the Netherlands' imperial achievements, was built to house the ever-increasing collections. Permanent exhibitions on South East Asia, Oceania, Western Asia and North Africa, Africa, Latin America, Man and Environment and Music, Dance and Theatre are featured along with varied temporary exhibitions.

The Tropenmuseum collection currently holds more than 254,000 pieces, of which 155,000 are Material Culture (objects), 89,000 are Photographic material (photographs, albums, slides, negatives) and 10,000 are imagery (drawings, paintings and documents).

The Tropenmuseum Junior (Children's Museum) is aimed at the 6- to12-year-old age group, and the approach is very "hands-on", allowing visitors to explore and examine the exhibits. Other activities of interest to children include native dances and costumes.

Musical performances, dance and drama are presented in the KIT Theatre in the evenings. Exotic dishes and snacks are served in the Ekeko restaurant, and the museum shop sells treasures from around the world.

Above: The elaborate interior of the Tropenmuseum

- ✚ **83 D3**
- ✉ **Tropenmuseum**
  Linnaeusstraat 2
- ☎ 020 568 8200
- 🌐 www.tropenmuseum.nl
  www. tropenmuseumjunior.nl
  (children)
- 🕐 Daily 10–5, 5 Dec, 24 Dec, 31 Dec 10–3; closed 1 Jan, 30 Apr, 5 May, 25 Dec
- 💵 Moderate, children under 5 free
- 🚌 22; Tram: 3, 7, 9, 10, 14

Vakbondmuseum, De Burcht

Amsterdam has long been renowned as a diamond capital, and in 1894 the General Dutch Diamond Workers Union became the country's first, largest and wealthiest trade union in the Netherlands. Its headquarters, inspired by an Italian palazzo, was designed by H P Berlage, who also designed the Beurs stock exchange.

From outside the building resembles a castle or *burcht*, hence its nickname of "De Burcht".

✚ **83 C2**

✉ **Vakbondmuseum, De Burcht**
Henri Polaklaan 9

☎ **020 624 1166**

🌐 **www.deburcht-vakbondsmuseum.nl**

🕐 Tue–Fri 11–5, Sun 1–5; closed public hols

✋ Moderate

🚊 Tram: 6, 9, 14

🚉 51, 53 Waterlooplein stop

There is a tower with a diamond in the window, and the stairwell entrance resembles a drawbridge over a moat. This was once the heart of the city's famous diamond trade, but World War II put an end to all activities as most of the diamond cutters were of Jewish origin. A commemorative stone in the foyer is a silent reminder of this tragic period.

Today, De Burcht houses the Vakbondmuseum of Dutch trade unions, with displays of memorabilia, a permanent exhibition about the history of 100 years of Dutch trade unions. The building is an architectural gem, so even if its theme is not of particular interest, do walk into the lobby to see the interior. Sunlight streams through white and yellow glass and through glass floor tiles to its Mediterranean-style covered courtyard. The yellow, white and blue glazed brick walls glisten, and the colourful interior is graced by vaults, columns and balustrades. The huge hanging lamp, high in the glass cupola, dominates the most beautiful of Amsterdam's staircases.

In the stylish rooms are paintings by Richard Roland Holst, stained-glass windows, wood panelling and furniture designed by Berlage.

Above: Interior of the Vakbondmuseum

Verzetsmuseum

The Verzetsmuseum tells the fascinating story of the Dutch resistance workers and life in the Netherlands during World War II. Using authentic objects, rare wartime memorabilia and modern techniques, the Dutch Resistance Museum evokes a powerful impression of the atmosphere of the time.

Around 25,000 courageous people were involved in the resistance movement or *verzet*, risking their own lives to save others and to disrupt the activities of the Nazis during their occupation.

The resistance story is told chronologically from the rise of Fascism around 1930 to the fight against racism after the war.

An overall picture of Dutch society in the 30s gives visitors the experience of the shock of the unexpected German invasion, the ensuing oppression and the peoples' resistance to the occupation which gradually intensified as the war progressed. There is also the realisation that many experiences from this period still play a role in today's society. There are

individual examples that give a visitor further insight into the resistance movement. Displays also recall the clever means with which the Dutch resistance sought to impair the Nazi occupation.

The museum houses a large permanent exhibition, an auditorium, a study area, an exhibition space in the foyer and a room for temporary exhibitions. For visitors with a specific area of interest a number of subjects can be perused on the "Information Island".

On leaving the museum, follow Plantage Middenlaan, on the south side of the Artis Zoo, to see Muiderpoort at Alexanderplein, the city gate built in 1770, through which Napoleon entered Amsterdam in 1811.

Above: Exterior view of the Verzetsmuseum

✚ **83 C2**

✉ **Verzetsmuseum**
Plantage Kerklaan 61a

☎ 020 620 2535

🌐 **www.dutchresistance
museum.nl**

🕐 Tue–Fri 10–5, Sat–Mon
noon–5; closed 1 Jan,
30 Apr, 25 Dec

✋ Moderate

🚌 Tram: 6, 9, 14

🚊 51, 53 Waterlooplein stop

Waterlooplein Market

The giant flea market held in Waterlooplein is on the original site of the daily market in the city's Jewish quarter. You'll find just about everything in this popular, lively place from bric-a-brac to antiques, junk, funky and vintage clothes, army surplus, and much more.

The square was created in 1880 by filling in two canals: Leprozengracht and Houtgracht. The largest and the most important Jewish market in Amsterdam was held here from 1893 until 1941, ending with the persecution of Jews by the Nazis. After World War II, the Waterlooplein market was revived as a marketplace and became a magnet for youth culture. It is the most popular market in the city.

The Stadhuis (City Hall) is part of a complex of buildings that includes the Muziektheater, home to the Dutch national opera and ballet companies. The two buildings are known collectively as Stopera (stadhuis + opera). The red brick, marble and glass complex is connected by an arcade with a mural depicting "Amsterdam's Peil" (city below sea-level). Its white marble panelling has earned it the nickname "false teeth". The Stopera caused quite a controversy when it was built. The construction site required the destruction of dozens of medieval houses that stood in the old Jewish Quarter.

Completed in 1988, the Musiektheater is the largest auditorium in the country with 1,689 seats (Waterlooplein 22; tel: box office 020 625 5455; www.muziektheater. nl; box office open 2 Jul–19 Aug, Mon–Fri 10–6; rest of year Mon–Fri 8:30am– 3:30pm, Thu 5–7pm; box office closed Sat–Sun). Free half-hour concerts are held on Tuesday lunchtimes from September to May, beginning at 12:30pm. Backstage tours take place on Saturdays at 3pm throughout the year.

Above: A few of the huge selection of curios on sale at the Waterlooplein flea market

✚ **83 A2**

✉ **Waterlooplein Market**
Waterlooplein

🕐 Mon–Fri 9–5, Sat 8:30–5:30

✋ Free

🚌 Tram: 9, 14

🚇 51, 53, 54 Waterlooplein stop

Zuiderkerk

Zuiderkerk was designed in 1603 by city architect Hendrik de Keyser, who also built the Noorderkerk and Westerkerk. He is buried here in the church. It was the first Protestant church built in Amsterdam after the Alteration and was completed in 1614.

Built in the Renaissance style, the splendid spire with its decorative free standing columns, ornate clocks and onion dome crown with a weather vane, is a prominent city landmark.

In 1929, the Zuiderkerk no longer functioned as a church. During the famine years of World War II, it needed to be used as a morgue. It also served as a storage depot for bibles. In 1944, an average of 50 corpses were brought in daily. In 1988 the church was restored and is now an information centre for urban development and renewal for the city's public housing department, with interesting architectural exhibitions.

You can listen to the tower's 35-bell carillon at noon on Thursdays and climb its 70m (265 feet) tower between June and September for a spectacular view (check opening times before your visit).

Nearby is Christ Church (Groenburgwal 42; tel: 020 624 8877; www.christchurch. nl) located on one of the city's most beautiful canals, the Groenburgwal, situated just off Staalstraat, between Zuiderkerk and the Amstel river. The Anglican Chaplaincy in Amsterdam was founded more than 300 years ago, in April 1698, when the Reverend John Cockburn DD was appointed as the English Episcopal Chaplain. Services are still held in the charming little church every Sunday at 10am.

Below: The colourful clockface on the soaring spire, complete with Ionic columns, of Zuiderkirk

✚ **83 A1**

✉ **Zuiderkerk**
Zuiderkerkhof 72

☎ 020 552 7987

www.zuiderkerk. amsterdam.nl

🕐 Mon–Fri 9–4, Sat noon–6; Apr–Sep every 30 mins tower climb

✋ Free

🚌 Tram: 4, 16, 24, 25 Dam stop, 9, 14 Waterlooplein stop

🚇 51 Nieuwmarkt stop

Museum Quarter

Some of the most important museums in the Netherlands are situated close together in this part of town. The wonderful Rijksmuseum national gallery, excellent Van Gogh Museum and Stedelijk Museum (closed for renovation until the end of 2008) are all in the spacious Museumplein park. Alternatively, you can shop in PC Hooftstraat, Amsterdam's most exclusive shopping street, or go bargain hunting at the famous Albert Cuyp open market. Vondelpark and Sarphatipark are perfect places for a quiet break from browsing and a picnic, or you could take in a classic movie at the Nederlands Filmmuseum. There are also museums devoted to Coster Diamonds, Heineken beer and Bols Dutch gin. Music and entertainment abound – from the Concertgebouw to the Stadsschouwburg theatre, Leidseplein street performers and open-air music concerts, together with gambling at Holland Casino, and shows at the comedy theatre. There's plenty to keep you entertained, whatever your taste.

MUSEUM QUARTER WALK

1. Leidseplein
See page 108

Begin on lively Leidseplein, where the Stadsschouwburg theatre (page113) and the art deco Amsterdam-American Hotel are located. Pass by the Holland Casino (page 107) and cross the bridge in front of the Marriott Hotel to Stadhouderskade. Turn right into tranquil Vondelpark.

2. Vondelpark
See page 116

In Vondelpark is the Nederlands Filmmuseum. Along the path which goes around the pond is Het Blauwe Theehuis, a round, blue teahouse. Retrace your steps back to the Filmmuseum, and walk over to the Vondelkerk, a former church that resembles a castle. To the left of Vondelkerk is the Hollandsche Manege, one of Europe's last and most beautiful city riding schools.

3. Museumplein Museums
See pages 110 & 114

Turn right into 1e Constantijn Huygenstraat and take the third left into Peter Cornelius Hoofdstraat, better known as P C Hoofdstraat, with its marvellous stores. Towards the end of the street turn right into Hobbemastraat for a great view across Museumplein, and for the national gallery, the Rijksmuseum (page 110), Van Gogh Museum (page 114) and the Stedelijk Museum for contemporary art (closed for renovation until the end of 2008).

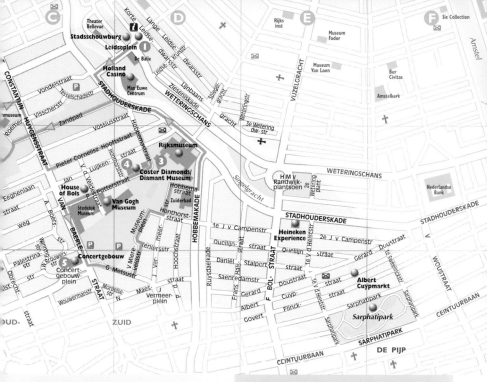

4. Diamant Museum
See page 104

Turning right along the Paulus Potterstraat, you will pass by Coster Diamonds diamond cutting and polishing workshop and the newly opened (2007) Diamant Museum (page 104). Have a look at their glistening displays. Amsterdam is famed as a city of diamonds and there is something for every taste and budget.

5. Concertgebouw
See page 103

Turn right onto Van Baerlestraat and pass by the glass-enclosed Concertgebouw concert hall, where some of the world's finest musicians entertain discerning music lovers. Paths criss-crossing Museumplein return you to the Rijksmuseum. Take Hobbemakade to Stadhouderskade, and turn left to return to Leidseplein (page 108) for a break in one of the cafés.

Albert Cuypmarket

The Albert Cuypmarket has been trading since 1904, and is the city's largest, best-known and least expensive commodity market. Food from around the world, fish, poultry, cheese, exotic fruits, vegetables as well as clothing, shoes, flowers, textiles and household goods are just some of the items on sale from its 325 stalls.

This wide street, once a canal, is named after Dutch landscape painter Albert Cuyp (1620–1691). It is located in the Pijp district, just behind the Heineken Experience and across Ferdinand Bolstraat.

On busy days the colourful, bustling market attracts well over 20,000 bargain hunters and almost twice as many shoppers on Saturdays. Stalls filled to the brim, music playing, the smell of food, laughter and friendly merchants make the atmosphere delightful. Speciality shops surround the world-famous market and cafés, and visitors can choose from an international assortment of goods and services. The market is not very crowded in the morning, but gets packed as the day progresses. In the late afternoon, food is sold off at bargain prices as stall-holders attempt to dispose of their remaining wares before returning home. Don't be afraid to bargain, but do watch out for pickpockets. The popularity of this market, with its reasonable prices and extensive supply of exotic goods, is due in part to the influx of writers, students and immigrants into the surrounding neighbourhoods.

Below: A stall-holder sells fresh produce in the Albert Cuyp street market

- ✚ **101 E3**
- ✉ **Albert Cuypmarket**
  Albert Cuypstraat
- 🌐 **www.albertcuypmarkt. com**
- 🕐 Mon–Sat 9–6
- 🖐 Free
- 🚋 Tram: 4 Stadhouderskade stop; 16, 24, 25 Albert Cuypstraat stop

Concertgebouw Concert Hall

The neo-Renaissance Concertgebouw, built in 1888, is known to music lovers throughout the country for its divine acoustics. Despite having no knowledge of music, architect A L van Gendt (1835–1901) designed one of the most acoustically sound concert halls in the world.

The versatile and popular architect based his plan on the design of the oval room of the Felix Meritis theatre (see page 180) to create a splendid building for the Royal Concertgebouw Orchestra. Many acclaimed orchestras and ensembles have performed here and many young musicians have made their debut in the main concert hall, Grote Zaal, and the smaller Kleine Zaal. The inaugural concert here featured 120 musicians and a 600-person choir.

The elaborate exterior has a colonnaded façade and is decorated with busts of composers, some muses and a gleaming harp atop the roof pinnacle.

Most noteworthy is the glass and steel enclosed extension designed by Pi de Bruijn which was added in 1983. The building was in danger of collapse when the supporting piles were afflicted with severe dry rot. In order to save the concert hall, the entire superstructure was lifted off the ground. The original underground wooden piles, resting on sand 13m (43 feet) below, were replaced by concrete piles that were sunk to a new depth of 18m (59 feet).

The original entrance was moved to the side of the building and the new glass extension with its cafés and meeting areas is integrated with the old building.

Above: The impressive façade of the Concertgebouw

✚ **101 C3**

✉ **Concertgebouw Concert Hall**
Concertgebouwplein 2–6,

☎ 020 671 8345

🌐 **www.concertgebouw.nl**

🕐 Box office daily 10–5

✋ Expensive, depending on event

🚌 170; Tram: 2, 3, 5, 12, 16, 24

Diamant Museum, Coster Diamonds

Amsterdam has been a city of diamonds since the 16th century. Four centuries of expertise have made the city a centre of diamond manufacturing and trading that is renowned the world over. Coster Diamonds was founded in 1840 and was the first diamond firm in Holland to use steam-powered machines to cut and polish the stones.

The firm was honoured by the British Crown by being chosen for the task of re-polishing the fabulous Koh-I-Noor (Mountain of Light) diamond in 1852. The famous 108.8 carat blue-white stone is one of the treasures of the British crown jewels and graces the coronation crown. A replica of the enormous jewel is on display in Coster's entrance foyer.

Free guided tours to see the talented diamond-cutters grading, cutting and polishing the stones attract thousands of people daily. Goldsmiths and diamond-cutters work together to produce a wide range of exquisite jewellery. Most diamonds are accompanied by a certificate of authenticity from the Gemological Institute of America or the Diamond High Council.

Three adjoining villas make up the Coster complex and, in 2007, Coster Diamonds opened the Amsterdam Diamant Museum, featuring the history of diamonds and a beautiful collection of jewels.

The exhibition begins with a short film that follows the diamond from its formation

deep within the earth 3 billion years ago, on its journey via mining, distribution, trade and processing to the splendid jewel adorning a neck, wrist or finger. You can view displays of crystals and the art of placing a diamond in a piece of jewellery. The exhibition also explains with examples the influence of the "4 Cs" (carat, clarity, colour and cut) on the valuation of the polished diamond.

Perhaps the most attractive display in the museum is the history of the world's 22 most famous diamonds, with their replicas on view. Famous diamond heists – some real and some reconstructed from film plots – are also documented.

If you still have any doubts why these sparkling stones continue to dazzle, don't miss the diamond-shaped mirror room.

Above left: Glittering replicas of the Crown Jewels; **above right:** The story of diamonds is told in the museum

Diamant Museum

✚ **101 D2**

✉ **Diamant Museum**
Paulus Potterstraat 8

☎ 020 305 5300/5301

🌐 **www.diamantmuseumamsterdam.nl**

🕐 Daily 9–5

✋ Moderate

Coster Diamonds

✉ **Coster Diamonds**
Paulus Potterstraat 2–8

☎ 020 305 5555

🌐 **www.costerdiamonds.com**

🕐 Daily 9–5; closed 25 Dec

✋ Free workshop tours

🚌 Tram: 2, 5 Hobbemastraat stop

Heineken Experience

The former Heineken brewery, now a museum, is a favourite stop for beer lovers. Beer was brewed here for 120 years before brewing moved to new premises in Zoeterwoude and Den Bosch in 1988. At the Heineken Experience you can see what it's like to make, bottle and deliver beer, and also enjoy some of the product.

In 1863, the young Gerard Heineken boldly risked the family fortune to take over the 16th-century Hooiberg (haystack) brewery and subsequently turned it into Amsterdam's most profitable brewery. The rest, as they say, is history. Heineken has become an international brand with more than 130 breweries in 65 countries, as well as some 170 locally brewed brands. In the historic complex you can learn about the tradition and craft of making delicious pilsner beer, explore malt grain silos and see what happens in the large copper kettles during the brewing process. Visit the stables and test your strength in handling a team of Shire horses, the drays that pulled the beer wagons in former times. The museum features "rides" and interactive exhibits. It also gives an insight into the company's history and their decades of advertising campaigns. The company claims that the original Heineken recipe has not changed since the beer was first produced nearly 150 years ago. A highlight for many visitors is the three complimentary glasses of Heineken. There are two bars, "Brewhouse" and "See You Again", where you can enjoy the famous brew with visitors from around the world. The gift shop is stocked with plenty of Heineken souvenirs and beer memorabilia.

Below: An elaborate golden beer tankard with fine, detailed engraving displayed in the museum

✚ **101 E2**

✉ **Heineken Experience**
Stadhouderskade 78

☎ 020 523 9666

🌐 **www.heineken experience.com**

🕐 Jun–Aug, daily 11–7 (last ticket 5:45); Sep–Oct, Tue–Sun 10–6 (last ticket 5)

✋ Expensive, children under 18 with parental guidance

🚊 Tram: 16, 24, 25 Heinekenplein on Stadhouderskade stop

Holland Casino

Holland Casino in Amsterdam is one of Europe's largest casinos. Try your hand at the usual games such as poker and roulette and a host of the more unusual, or take a chance on Sic Bo, a Chinese dice game.

Gambling has been legal in the Netherlands since 1975. There are 38 cities in the Netherlands with a total of 50 casinos. In 2004, following a reallocation of responsibilities between government departments, the Ministry of Finance assumed the role of "sole shareholder" in Holland Casino on behalf of the State. The casinos are a major source of tax revenue for the country, so even if you don't win, others do, albeit indirectly. There are also special ladies nights and dinner shows. You must be 18 and present your passport; there is no strict dress code.

The House of Bols

The House of Bols is all about *jenever*, also known as Dutch gin. Founded in Amsterdam in 1575, Bols is the world's oldest distiller, producing *jenever* since 1664. *Jenever* is the juniper-flavoured and strongly alcoholic traditional liquor of the Netherlands and Flanders, from which gin has evolved. It was first sold as a medicine in the late 16th century.

Rembrandt and founder Lucas Bols were neighbours, and Rembrandt once paid his bill with a painting by one of his students. The House of Bols Museum consists of two floors in the new Amsterdam headquarters of Bols. In the museum, you can learn about *jenever*, liqueurs and cocktails and see how *jenever* used to be produced in copper kettles.

Above right: Outside the Holland Casino

Holland Casino

✚ **101 D1**

✉ **Holland Casino**
Max Eeuwplein 62

☎ 020 521 1111

🌐 **www.hollandcasino.com**

🕐 Daily noon–3am

🚋 Tram: 1, 2, 3, 5 Leideseplein stop

House of Bols

✚ **101 C2**

✉ **House of Bols**
Paulus Potterstraat 14

☎ 020 570 8575

🌐 **www.houseofbols.nl**

🕐 Wed–Mon noon–6

✋ Expensive

🚋 Tram: 2, 3, 5, 12 Van Baerlestraat stop; 16, 24 Museumplein stop

Leidseplein

Day or night, Leidseplein is buzzing with activity. Known as Amsterdam's liveliest square, it's filled with cafés, restaurants, street performers, neon lights, music and a party atmosphere. It's also a busy transport hub intersected by the tram lines that criss-cross the city.

The 17th-century square was formerly a wagon park for peasants and farmers, who would unload their carts here at the outskirts of the city. Named after the Leidsepoort city gate demolished in 1862, it has been a popular gathering place for centuries: for writers and artists, political factions in the 1930s, anti-Nazi rallies during 1940s, protest groups in the 1960s and celebrations in 1992 following local football team Ajax's UEFA Cup victory. It's also the place to be for New Year's Eve celebrations.

By day the square is a hub of activity with performances by fire-eaters, human-statues, mime artists and musicians filling the air with a variety of sounds from around the globe.

At night it is transformed into a hot-spot, with fun-seekers bathed in the glow of neon lights enjoying drinks on the crowded terraces that seat more than 1,000 people. You'll also find a casino, more bars, restaurants, night clubs and cinemas on and around the Leidseplein going strong until the early hours. The Amsterdam-American hotel with its art deco Café Américain dating back to 1904, the Stadsschouwburg (Municipal Theatre) from 1894 with its distinctive red-brick façade and the Leidseplein Theatre are all here. Watch out for drunken tourists and pickpockets.

✚ 101 D1

⊠ Leidseplein
City centre

⊕ Daily

⊟ Tram: 1, 2, 5, 6, 7, 10

⊟ Museum boat: Stop 5

Above: Leidseplein buzzes with nightlife in the evening; **left:** The bronze bust of an austere Arthur van Schindel, set in a tree-lined park near Amsterdam's Leidseplein

Rijksmuseum – National Gallery

The world-famous Rijksmuseum possesses an unparalleled collection of Dutch art from the 15th to the 19th century. It is the largest museum in the Netherlands and contains some 7 million items. Part of the museum is currently undergoing renovation.

The main collection, and national pride, is the 17th-century work of the Dutch masters of the Golden Age. Rembrandt's impressive, dramatic canvas *The Night Watch* – one of his largest and most famous paintings – portrays an Amsterdam militia company in 1642, and is a showpiece of the period. His painting *The Jewish Bride* as well as works painted by his students are also shown. Several paintings by Johannes Vermeer, known for his attention to detail and portrayal of space and light, are represented including *The Milk Maid* and *The Love Letter*. Haarlem artist Frans Hals, known for his lively portraits and Jan Steen with his humorous depictions of daily life, also feature prominently.

In addition, elegant period rooms display Old Dutch silver, Delftware porcelain, glassware, furniture and decorations, which recall the glories of the Golden Age. In Sculpture and the Applied Arts, there is jewellery and other objects d'art along with numerous treasures, including two

doll's houses modelled on canal houses, complete in every detail. Dutch History is the story of the nation as told through paintings. The 18th- and 19th-century Dutch paintings showcase a fine collection of portraits, landscapes and still lifes.

The Dutch Impressionists of The Hague school from circa 1870 feature a group of artists known for their atmospheric landscape paintings capturing the subdued sunlight of the grey Dutch skies.

A self-guided audio tour is available in English, as well as a museum guidebook, and a brochure which points out some of the highlights of the Dutch Golden Age collection.

The Rijksmuseum is undergoing major refurbishment until 2008, and most of the building is closed. However, a display of 400 of the 17th-century masterpieces may be seen in the adjoining Phillips Wing to the rear of the main building, where artefacts, paintings and sculpture from the Asiatic Art collection are on display.

Above left: The distinctive Gothic façade of the Rijksmuseum building; **above right:** Staff in conversation at an entrance to the museum

➕ **101 D2**

✉ **Rijksmuseum – National Gallery**
Stadhouderskade 42

☎ 020 674 7000

🌐 **www.rijksmuseum.nl**

🕐 Daily 9–6 (also Fri 6–10pm)

💷 Moderate

🚋 Tram: 2, 5 Hobbemastraat stop;
7, 10 Spiegelgracht stop;
3, 12, 16, 24 Museumplein stop

🚤 Museum boat: Stop 6

Sarphati Park

The Sarphati Park is the perfect park for a rest after you've walked through the Albert Cuypmarket and done your shopping. You'll find people taking a leisurely stroll, jogging, walking their dogs, playing games or just enjoying the view.

Located near the Ceintuurbaan in the heart of the Oud Zuid in de Pijp district, this small, tranquil open space with its narrow lake is one of Amsterdam's most charming parks. It is also conveniently surrounded by cafés and snack bars.

A bronze bust of Dutch doctor, philanthropist and city planner Samuel Sarphati, after whom the park is named, stands in an elaborate fountain-ringed monument surrounded by grassy lawns. In the second half of the 19th century, there was a severe shortage of houses for workers due to the city's rapid growth. The gifted and socially

conscious Dr Sarphati was known as "the founder of modern Amsterdam." He envisioned the building of a spacious suburb with affordable housing for the middle- and working classes, with this beautiful park in the middle. It was partly implemented during his lifetime and completed after his death. Sarphati also built banks, a commercial

college, a construction company, a bread factory, organised refuse collection and transport and built the Amstel Hotel.

Sarphati Park is laid out in English landscape style and is surrounded by grand houses. It opened in 1885 and continues to offer the community respite and relaxation. It is a lovely place to escape the hectic city.

Right: Space to run free in Sarphati Park

🕂 **101 F3**

✉ **Sarphati Park**
Public park

🕐 Daily dawn–dusk

✋ Free

🚊 Tram: 16, 24, 25
Albert Cuypstraat stop;
3 Sarphatipark stop

Stadsschouwburg Theatre

Repertoires of both classical and modern plays are performed in the Stadsschouwburg, Amsterdam's municipal theatre. Renowned Dutch and international theatre companies perform a variety of musicals, dance and drama here.

The original plans for the red-brick exterior of this neo-Renaissance building included beautiful ornamentation, though it was never carried out due to budget cuts. A hostile public reaction to the building and to the theatre management's policy of allowing only patrons who had purchased the most expensive tickets to use the front door did not help its popularity. Until 1986 when the Muziektheater Stopera was completed (see page 96), the Stadsschouwburg was home to the Dutch national ballet and opera companies.

The first wooden municipal theatre opened in 1638 on Keizersgracht. For the opening, playwright Joost van de Vondel wrote *Gysbrecht van Aemstel* which became the traditional opening performance of the New Year for years to come. In 1772 the theatre burned down when twice as many candles as usual were used to illuminate the stage. A new theatre was built on Leideseplein but was also destroyed in a fire in 1890, caused by fireworks. The current building (1892) was designed by A L van Gendt and Jan Springer. Guided tours are available in English, by reservation.

A number of local groups such as the resident Toneelgroep Amsterdam stage plays, and English-language productions are presented annually by In-Players.

Above: Exterior view of the Stadsschouwburg Theatre

🕂 **101 D1**

✉ **Stadsschouwburg Theatre**
Leidseplein 26

☎ 020 624 2311

🌐 **www.stadsschouwburg amsterdam.nl**

🕓 Box office Mon–Sat, 10–6

✋ Expensive

🚋 Tram: 1, 2, 5, 6, 7, 10

🚤 Museum boat: Stop 5

Van Gogh Museum

The Van Gogh Museum contains the world's largest collection of works by Vincent Van Gogh (1853–1890) with more than 200 of his paintings, 500 drawings and 850 letters written to his brother Theo. Van Gogh's vivid, vibrant use of colour and his exuberant Impressionistic style draw visitors from around the world.

Van Gogh's tragic life and the development of his extraordinary style are traced through a combination of works from both the Dutch and French periods of Van Gogh's life, which was cut short by his suicide at the age of 37 when he shot himself. The core of the collection belonged to Theo who, although an art dealer, did not succeed in helping his brother to fame and fortune. Most of Van Gogh's best-known works are on display, as well as his fine collection of Japanese prints. The collection also includes works by many of Van Gogh's contemporaries, including Gauguin, Monet, Pissarro and Toulouse-Lautrec.

Van Gogh painted in the Netherlands for five years before moving to Paris in 1886. His broad brush strokes and bold colours show the influence of Impressionism on his work. He moved to Arles in 1888 after tiring of city life. The brilliant sunlight and intense hues of Provence intoxicated Van Gogh and

Vincent van Gogh
1853–1890

Above left: The modernist exterior of the Van Gogh Museum, **above right:** Visitors viewing a Van Gogh self-portrait

he painted some of his best works there, including *Sunflowers* and *Bedroom in Arles*.

Tormented by mental instability, Van Gogh voluntarily entered an asylum in St Remy after he had cut off a portion of his ear and offered it to a prostitute. Here his work became expressionistic. His mental anguish is apparent in paintings such as *Wheatfield and Crows* with its violent sky and menacing birds. In his lifetime, he sold only one painting.

The museum building is based on a design by De Stijl architect Gerrit Rietveld and was specially constructed in 1973 to house this collection, with Vincent Van Gogh's nephew acting as advisor.

The Stedelijk Museum next door (closed for renovation until the end of 2008; see page 136) contains international paintings and sculptures dating from 1850 to the present, and post-1945 art.

✚ **101 C2**

✉ **Van Gogh Museum**
Paulus Potterstraat 7

☎ 020 570 5200

🌐 **www.vangoghmuseum.nl**

🕐 Daily 10–6 (also Fri 10–10)

💷 Expensive

🚌 145, 170, 172; Tram: 2, 3, 5, 12 Van Baerlestraat stop

Vondelpark

Vondelpark is the most well-known, most visited and the largest park in Amsterdam. The park is a popular place for walking, jogging, skating and other sports, listening to music, sunbathing and people-watching, and there are also plenty of attractions.

Designed in an English landscape style by the architect L D Zocher and his son, the park gives the illusion of a perfectly natural 19th-century countryside landscape. With its open spaces, grassy fields, formal rose garden, ornamental lakes, meadows and woodland containing more than 120 varieties of trees, the 48ha (118-acre) park became the heart of a new residential district when it opened in 1865. The statue of Dutch playwright Joost van den Vondel (1587–1679) was erected in 1867. Paved paths, wooded trails, a children's paddling pool and playgrounds provide for hours of enjoyment. Vondelkerk was begun in 1872 and completed in 1880. A fire broke out in 1904 and the church was rebuilt, but deconsecrated in 1979 and in 1985 was converted into offices.

Het Blauwe Theehuis

The round, blue pagoda-like circular café on two levels was built in 1937 in the style of the Amsterdam School and has an upstairs balcony terrace as well as a park-level terrace, the largest in the city, for 800 people. The teahouse is a popular lunch spot. Upstairs is a stylish bar with a DJ on Friday evenings and live music on Sundays.

Nederlands Filmmuseum

The Film Museum is the national centre for cinematography in the Netherlands. More than 1,000 new and classic films are shown annually. The art deco interior is the original interior of Amsterdam's first cinema, Cinema Parisien. Films begin at 8:15pm and Café Vertigo is popular for refreshments.

Vondelpark

✚ **100 A2**

✉ **Vondelpark**
Bordered by Overtoom, Stadhouderskade and PC Hooftstraat

🕐 Daily dawn–dusk

✋ Free

🚊 Tram: 1, 2, 3, 5, 6, 12

Hollandsche Manege

One of Europe's last and most beautiful city riding schools, dating from 1882, is based on the Spanish riding school in Vienna. Decorative horse heads grace the façade. Watch the equestrians practising and enjoy the lovely café. The school provides riding in the Amsterdamse Bos.

Vondelpark Openluchttheater

Free summer concerts, drama, cabaret and children's activities are performed her from the beginning of July to mid-August. There are 1,500 seats spread over three stands.

Above left: A peaceful spot for relaxing in Vondelpark; **below:** Statue of the playwright Vondel

Film MHet Blauwe Theehuis

✉ **Het Blauwe Theehuis**
(Blue Tea house), Vondelpark 5

☎ 020 662 0254

🌐 www.blauwetheehuis.nl

🕓 Lunch daily 10–4; Dinner daily 6–10; Brunch Thu 9–11, Fri–Sat 9–1

Nederlands Filmmuseum

✉ **Nederlands Filmmuseum**
Vondelpark

☎ 3 020 589 1400

🌐 www.filmmuseum.nl

🕓 Mon–Fri 9am–10:15pm, Sat–Sun opens 1 hour before 1st performance until 10:15pm

🚋 Tram: 12 Overtoom stop

Hollandsche Manege

✉ **Hollandsche Manege**
Vondelstraat 140

☎ 020 618 0942

🌐 www.dehollandschemanege.nl

🕓 Mon–Fri 9am–11pm, Sat 9–5, Sun 9–2

🚋 Tram: 1, 6

Vondelpark Openluchttheater

✉ **Vondelpark Openluchttheater**
(Office), Marnixstraat 427

☎ 020 523 7790 / 020 428 3360

🌐 www.openluchttheater.nl

🚋 Tram: 1, 2, 3, 6, 12

Eastern Docklands & IJ Harbour

Urban expansion in the area along the river IJ, behind Centraal Station, now forms an exciting new section of the city. It successfully blends the old and the new in converted warehouses, imaginative contemporary architecture and modern neighbourhoods on charming new islands. Then there's the new PTA passenger terminal, Muziekgebouw concert hall and hotels adding to the charm. You'll find sites of historical and cultural importance from the city's shipping past in the Scheepsvaartmuseum, Schreierstoren, Montelbaanstoren, Scheepvaarthuis, and the St Nicolaaskerk and Oosterkerk. Check out technological developments in NEMO and Werf 't Kromhout museum for voyages of discovery.

EASTERN DOCKLANDS & IJ HARBOUR WALK

1. St Nicolaaskerk
See page 134
Starting from St Nicolaaskerk, opposite Centraal Station (page 30), continue walking along Prins Hendrikkade waterfront. Pass the Schreierstoren or (Tower of Tears), where families wept for their loved ones departing on East India Company ships and for those who had been long at sea (page 133).

2. NEMO Science and Technology Museum
See page 128
In front of you to the left extending out over the water of Oosterdok is NEMO Science and Technology Museum – a large, green, boat-shaped building, with plenty of hands-on and interactive exhibits. The IJ tunnel that crosses under the IJ river runs underneath the building.

3. ARCAM Amsterdam Centre for Architecture
See page 122
Continuing on Prins Hendrikkade, you will pass the Scheepvaarthuis building (page 131) on your way to the ARCAM architecture centre. At ARCAM you can see some of the incredible designs of various new buildings as well as learning about the progress of renovation projects in the old city. As the city grows, more expansion is planned.

4. Nederlands Scheepvaartmuseum
See page 132
Around the corner is the Nederlands Scheepvaartmuseum, the Dutch Maritime Museum, once the arsenal of the Dutch Navy. The *Amsterdam* (left) is usually moored here, but during renovations to the museum it is moored at NEMO. Retrace your steps towards ARCAM and turn left onto Kadijksplein which runs along Schippersgracht canal.

5. Werf 't Kromhout Museum
See page 138
Turn left and walk along Entrepotdok quay. Continue to Entreepot Sluis then cross over to the Werf 't Kromhout Museum on Kadijk, one of the few remaining shipyards. At the end of the quay is the De Gooyer Windmill (page 139). Cross the bridge onto Oostenburgergracht to reach the 17th-century Oosterkerk. In front of the church, Kattenburgergracht leads into Prins Hendrikkade and back to St Nicolaaskerk and Central Station.

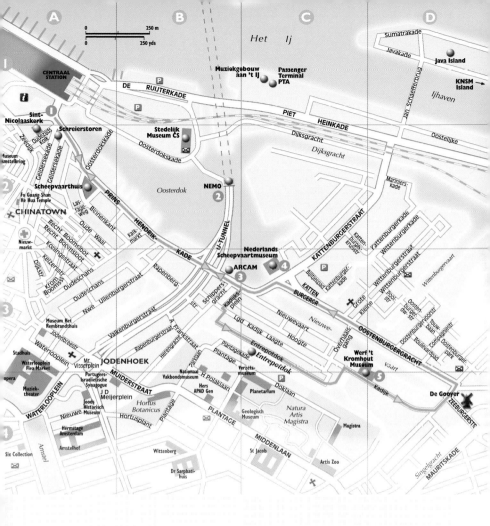

ARCAM – Amsterdam Centre for Architecture

The Amsterdam Centre for Architecture has focused its activities since 1986 on broadening architecture's appeal to a wider audience. ARCAM is a service centre with exhibitions about architecture, urbanism and landscape architecture. This is where architecture aficionados can get information about interesting sites throughout the city.

The exhibition programme is varied and highlights architects, buildings, urban developments, architectural themes and architecture abroad. On average, five exhibitions are organised annually on topical issues. Lectures, discussions, public debates and other events are also on the programme. ARCAM Panorama shows you the history of architecture from AD800 to the present. The centre can connect you with excursion operators specialising in both historical and modern Amsterdam architecture, which can be seen by foot, bicycle or boat, as well as direct you to architectural centres, specialised architecture bookshops, spatial planning, art and architecture courses and more, including garden design and landscape architecture.

ARCAM publishes an architectural guide containing information on a large (and still growing) number of Amsterdam buildings, most of them post-1940. Among the topics that it addresses is, for example, the significance of various buildings dating from a particular period of time – for example, Nieuwe Kerk was built around the same time as the Duomo in Florence, and the Waag was built as a city gate shortly before Columbus discovered America. This knowledge adds a different dimension to understanding what makes Amsterdam what it is today – a mixture of cultures and styles.

ARCAM's website features a digital map of Amsterdam, a timeline and a search facility to find information on city architecture. ARCAM's Archishuttle series was developed for use on public transport, drawing the passengers' attention to urban design and architecture along the route. There is, of course, much more information available in Dutch than in the English language but what is available is enough to introduce you to the varied architecture of the city.

Left: ARCAM – a building fit for an architecture exhibition

✚ **121 B3**

✉ **ARCAM - Amsterdam Centre for Architecture**
Prins Hendrikkade 600

☎ 020 620 4878

🌐 **www.arcam.nl**

🕐 Tue–Sat 1–5; closed Mon, Sun and public hols

✋ Free

🚋 22 Kadijkplein

🚢 Museum boat: Stop 6

Entrepot Dock

The former East India Company warehouses on the quayside of
the Entrepot Dock have undergone one of the city's most striking
metamorphoses. The buildings have been converted into a wonderful
assortment of homes, offices and restaurants. Many original façades
have been preserved, retaining the "Dutchness" of the dockland skyline.

The warehouse interiors have been opened
up to make inner courtyards and some of
the warehouses were so deep that an inner
passage was put through the middle to let
in light and air at first-floor level.

A neoclassical arch at one end of the
dock marks the entrance to what was

once the port. Goods coming from exotic
countries were stored here until the required
excise duties had been paid. There are 84
monumental warehouses, all named after
Dutch and Belgian cities, which are still
shown on name plaques on the fronts of
the buildings.

Amsterdam's dockland area held the greatest complex of warehouses in Europe in the mid-19th century and was also a customs-free zone for goods in transit in the city's busy port.

The East India Company (VOC) and the Admiralty joined together in building shipyards, warehouses and rope-making factories to meet the demands of supplying and maintaining both the shipbuilding industry and the military fleet.

The VOC employed more than a thousand workers in the shipyards. Piles of wood lay in the water for six months until sufficiently leached for construction; thereafter it took about 18 months to complete a boat from start to finish.

Above left and right: Entrepot Dock, a vast complex of converted warehouses

✚ **121 C3**

✉ **Entrepot Dock**

🕓 Daily

✋ Free

🚌 22, 43 Oostenburgergracht stop; 42 Kadijksplein stop; Tram: 6, 9, 14, 22, 32

Java and KNSM Islands

Increasing city expansion has given Amsterdam new architecture and stunning urban design in the Eastern Docklands area. The history, contemporary buildings and harbour landscape make for an inviting area to walk and explore, or to take a guided tour. KNSM Island was constructed at the end of the 19th century for the Royal Dutch Steamboat Company (Koninklijke Nederlandse Stoomboot Maatschappij – KNSM). It is known for its monumental buildings and residential towers.

The architects kept in mind the character of the old port when designing buildings for this island and produced imaginative architecture with international élan. Conservation was an important consideration, and so the old and the new merge beautifully.

Java Island has coloured buildings, gardens, small canals and quaint bridges. Nineteen young architects designed the extraordinary houses. They divided the long island into four sections, and dug four narrow canals.

These islands are part of the Oostelijke Eilanden (Eastern Islands) in the eastern reaches of the harbour, where there is a demand for housing for people wishing to live outside the city centre.

The fantasy-rich pedestrian and traffic bridges are a work of art. What you see is a modern version of old Amsterdam which retains the "feel" of the canal district, all buildings have variations but at the same time maintain a unified street frontage.

Independent urban designers have created some of the most exciting new constructions in this part of the city. The existing harbour basins have been preserved and harbour buildings renovated. Building both for the neighbourhood and the market – as well as for residents of different income levels – makes for a diverse and talented urban population. Each area has its particular allure.

After you disembark on Java Island, follow the northern quay and walk towards the area where there are older buildings, most of which are currently undergoing rigorous reconstruction. Try spotting gable stones depicting various maritime

images – clocks, spouts, bells, nymphs, ships, boats, animals – studded to the façade of the houses. Each of the houses on Java Island is individually designed and there is much to see so it's a good idea to hire a bicycle to explore the area.

Do visit the viewpoint at Venetiekade, from where you can admire the entrance to the Amsterdam-Rijnkanaal (the Amsterdam-Rhine Canal) and Oranjesluizen (Orange Locks) that connect Amsterdam to the IJ lake.

During the 1970s this area was made up of artists, city nomads and houseboat dwellers living around the vacant warehouses. For this reason, the area still has a fairly bohemian character.

At nearby Levantkade you can relax after your explorations at one of the many open-air cafés and restaurants that overlook the barges and docks. The most famous is Kanis en Meiland at No. 127; the name is a clever Dutch word play on KNSM-Eiland.

✚ **121 D1**

✉ **Java and KNSM Islands**

Muziekgebouw aan 't IJ

Music lovers should head to the waterfront, the meeting place on the newly developed banks of the IJ and the old heart of the city. The Muziekgebouw aan 't IJ is hailed as the concert hall of the 21st century.

The glass building appears to be moored on the quayside like a large transparent ship. Designed by the Danish architectural firm 3xNielesen, the €52 million construction is an international showpiece for the city. Musicians, composers and audiences alike can enjoy this building with plenty of space, multiple auditoriums with moveable walls, rehearsal spaces and offices for ensembles and music organisations.

Muziekgebouw aan 't IJ

- 121 C1
- ✉ **Muziekgebouw aan 't IJ**
  Piet Heinkade 1
- ☎ 020 788 2000
- 🌐 **www.muziekgebouw.nl**
- 🕐 Box office Mon–Sat noon–7
- ✋ Expensive
- 🚊 Tram: 25, 26 Muziekgebouw-Bimhuis stop

NEMO

Experience an imaginative and entertaining voyage of discovery at NEMO. Formerly known as New Metropolis Science and Technology Centre, it attracts people of all ages. Unlike at most museums, here you are encouraged to follow one rule: do touch everything and explore!

The word "Nemo" itself means "nobody", the idea behind the name being that visitors will believe themselves to be in no-man's land where fantasy suddenly becomes real much like the tales of Jules Verne, which inspired the name. The building itself is fantastical, resembling a large blue-green ship moored on the quay.

NEMO appeals to the child in every age group and it's a very "hands-on" place. The philosophy of its design is that the best way to learn is "to do". Business, technology, energy, science and human emotions are all dealt with in various interactive displays which are educational and fun. There are also shows that explain, among other things, the science of juggling!

Skylights and staircases visually link the interior levels. All displays and interactive projects are presented in English and Dutch. In "Wonder Lab" you step into the shoes of a scientist and carry out all kinds of experiments. "Why the World Works" is a collection of exhibits on electricity, magnetism, light and colour, while "Journey through the Mind" provides an interactive gallery on psychology, cognition and the brain. In "Code Name DNA" see how heredity works and in "Water Worlds" explore the technology behind clean drinking water. Another exhibition titled "Amazing Constructions" shows how the knowledge of form, shape and mechanics helps us to build structures.

The giant green building was designed by the Italian architect Renzo Piano who also designed the Centre Pompidou in Paris and the Kansai airport terminal at Osaka, Japan.

In summer the top-floor restaurant and the roof terrace offer a fabulous deck to catch the sun and appreciate great vistas of the city and the surrounding harbour. So even if you are not interested in the museum, do come here for a magnificent view of Amsterdam city.

The gift store is filled with educational toys and souvenirs. NEMO also develops educational products, projects and games by creating lecture programmes, demonstrations and workshops.

While the nearby Scheepvaartmuseum (see page 132) is undergoing renovations, its ship *Amsterdam* is moored at the quay beside NEMO.

Left: The green copper hull of the NEMO Museum

✚ **121 B2**

✉ **NEMO**
Oosterdok 2

☎ 020 531 3233

🖥 **www.e-nemo.nl**

🕐 Sep–Jun, Tue–Sun 10–5; Jul–Aug and school hols, daily 10–5; closed 1 Jan, 30 Apr, 25 Dec

✋ Expensive

🚌 22, 43 Kadijksplein stop

Passenger Terminal Amsterdam PTA

Passenger Terminal Amsterdam PTA lies on the southern bank of the IJ river, where the new expansion is changing the city's skyline on either side of Centraal Station. The bold, wave-like structure and the interior promenade deck give the building a nautical air.

With the focus mostly on tourism during summer months, ocean and river cruise passengers receive a warm reception at the terminal which is a showpiece for the capital. PTA also serves as an event location. Under the undulating roof of this imaginatively designed building is a large space for events – spread over three levels – which can accommodate 3,000 guests. The façade with its abundance of glass provides for a magnificent view over IJ harbour and the city.

The striking building has a 600m (660-yard) long quay, a terminal for touring cars, offices, a convention centre and a subterranean parking with 500 parking places. At one end of the terminal are the IJ Tower, restaurant Fifteen and offices.

Passenger Terminal Amsterdam is a joint venture between the Port of Amsterdam, which looks after the maritime operation, and NS Stations, which is responsible for managing and marketing the terminal. In a well-conceived development, living, working and recreation go hand in hand in a modern urban environment within the immediate environs of the old city centre. With a water-side line-up that includes the Muziekgebouw, Bimhuis Jazz, NEMO, the new Mövenpick Hotel and the Scheepvaart Maritime Museum, there is plenty to keep visitors entertained. This new section of Amsterdam will be completed by 2012.

Above: A view of the wave-like Passenger Terminal PTA

✚ **121 C1**

✉ **Passenger Terminal Amsterdam PTA**
Piet Heinkade 27

☎ 020 509 1000

🌐 **www.ptamsterdam.nl**

🕐 Daily

✋ Free

🚊 Tram: 25 Passenger Terminal Amsterdam stop; 26 Muziekgebouw stop

Scheepvaarthuis

The Scheepvaarthuis (Shipping House) was originally commissioned by six shipping companies to house their offices. It is appropriately named for a building that overlooks the Oosterdok (Eastern Dock).

The building is considered to be the first constructed in the true architectural style of the Amsterdam School, characteristics of which are the profuse masonry along the chimneys, ridge beams and frames and the design of the corners. Built between 1912 and 1916, Scheepvaarthuis was designed by architect J M van der Mey and his colleagues who were students of one of the leading Dutch architects, Cuypers (Centraal Station, Rijksmuseum).

The tapered triangular form of the building suggests the bow of a ship, and is adorned with a statue of the sea god Neptune, his wife and four female figures, each representing one of the points of the compass.

The impressive building is decked with marine-themed decorations such as dolphins, seahorses, waves and anchors and is richly adorned with sculptures, wrought iron and exotic wood. The remarkable central stairwell features shells, octopus and other nautical figures. The four oceans (Indian Ocean, the Mediterranean, the Pacific and Atlantic Ocean) are represented around the entrance where the stained-glass window of Neptune is depicted with a globe. In the other window, the cities of Amsterdam and Venice symbolise the Dutch East India Company and the Dutch West India Company. The glass canopy beautifully lights the atrium. The last shipping company left the building

in 1981 and in 1983 the GVB municipality transport company moved in. Now there are plans to make it a hotel.

Above: Boats and barges moor at the quayside in front of the Scheepvaarthuis

---

✚ **121 A2**

✉ **Scheepvaarthuis**
Prins Hendrikkade
108–114

🕐 Currently closed for renovation

🚊 22, 42, 43; Tram: 1, 2, 4, 5, 9, 13, 16, 17, 20, 24, 25

Scheepvaartmuseum – Netherlands Maritime Museum

The glorious seafaring history of the Netherlands is presented with nautical flair in the former arsenal of the Dutch Navy. The most popular exhibit is a replica of the 18th-century sailing ship *Amsterdam*. The museum is closed for renovation, but the ship remains open to the public, currently moored next to NEMO (see page 129).

✚ **121 C3**

✉ **Scheepvaartmuseum – Netherlands Maritime Museum**
Kattenburgerplein 1

☎ 020 523 2222

🌐 **www.scheepvaart museum.nl**

🕐 Currently closed for renovation

🚌 22, 43 Kattenburgplein stop

The original Dutch East Indiaman sank off the English coast in 1749 during its maiden voyage. You can climb aboard this giant three-master and from April to October watch the crew (of actors) swab the decks, sing sea shanties, load cargo, and also visit the crew's quarters.

The neoclassical building (1656) is constructed around a courtyard where artillery was stored. The building is supported by 18,000 piles driven into the ground of the Oosterdok. In 1973 it was converted into a museum containing the world's largest collection of ships.

In the museum Dutch maritime history is presented in a chronological order from before its 17th-century golden era, to 19th-century merchant shipping to the present, including technological developments. The *Royal Barge*, a beautifully constructed pleasure craft from 1818, built for King Willem I is displayed, along with magnificent ship models, artefacts, the first sea-atlas and world maps showing the Americas as they were then known.

Above: A tour boat is dwarfed by the *Amsterdam*

Schreierstoren

The Schreierstoren (Tower of Tears) is so named because tearful wives and girlfriends came here to wave goodbye to their seafaring men. Voyages often took up to four years and many sailors did not survive their journeys.

Possibly the name is not as romantic as the popular legend, but refers to the tower's location on a sharp 90-degree bend (screye or schorpe in Dutch) in the ancient town walls. A plaque depicts a weeping woman bearing the inscription scrayer hovck, meaning sharp corner. The tower was part of Amsterdam's medieval city walls and dates from 1480. One of the few remaining fortifications that were not demolished as the city expanded, it now houses the VOC Café. Located just behind the St Nicolaaskerk, the Schreierstoren was the point of departure for Dutch East Indies ships. A bronze plaque commemorates this as the spot where Henry Hudson departed on the Half

Moon in 1609, searching for a faster route to the East Indies. Instead he discovered the river that still bears his name in New York, which was formerly the settlement called Nieuw Amsterdam.

Above: The "Tower of Tears" with the entrance to Café VOC on the ground floor

Schreierstoren

✚ **121 A2**

✉ **Schreierstoren**
   Prins Hendrikkade 94–95

☎ 020 428 8291

▓ **www.schreierstoren.nl**

🕐 Mon 10–6, Tue 10–8, Wed–Thu 10–1, Fri–Sat 10–8, Sun noon–8

🚋 Tram: 1, 2, 4, 5, 9, 13, 16, 17, 24, 25

St Nicolaaskerk

St Nicholas is the patron saint of sailors. The prime location of the church next to the harbour and the Schreierstoren, served as a spiritual meeting point for seafarers and their families. The church of St Nicholas is one of the most beautifully decorated churches in Amsterdam, with

With its rich interior and imposing exterior, it was the most impressive of the churches built in 1887 after the 200-year ban on Catholic worship was lifted. Prior to that, the parish of St Nicolaaskerk met to worship at the "hidden" Catholic church of Lieve Heer op Solder (Our Lord in the Attic), now part of the Amstelkring museum (see page 22).

The official name of the church is St Nicolaas binnen de Veste (St Nicolas inside the Walls), referring to its location within the original walled city of Amsterdam.

The floor plan is a conventional three-aisled cruciform basilica church. Two towers with baroque-style spires grace the façade with a large rose window in between. In the centre is a bas relief depicting Jesus and the four Evangelists. The transept has polygonal closures on both sides, and at the crossing, the large octagonal tower is crowned with a baroque dome topped with a lantern-tower.

The Stichting Muziek in de Nicolaas (SMN – the Music Foundation of St Nicholas Church) was established in 2000 for the presentation of choral and instrumental music. Frequent concerts and choral services are held here. Performances on the Sauer organ (1889) are highlights of the cultural life of the city, given annually during the International Organ Concert Series in summer.

✚ **121 A2**

✉ **St Nicolaaskerk**
Prins Hendrikkade 73

☎ 020 624 8749 (Stichting Muziek in de Nicolaas)

🖥 **www.muziekindenic olaas.nl**
www.nicolaas-parochie.nl

🕒 Tue–Fri 11–4, Mon, Sat noon–3 (also Sep–Jul, Sat 5pm choral evensong in English, Sun 5pm Vespers in Latin)

✋ Free

🚊 Tram: 1, 2, 4, 5, 6, 9, 13, 16, 17, 24, 25

Below: Viewed from the canal, the towers and dome of St Nicolaaskerk

Stedelijk Museum CS

The Stedelijk is Amsterdam's foremost venue for contemporary art and one of the world's leading modern art museums. Some of the greatest names in art are exhibited in its internationally renowned collection.

Until the end of 2008 just a few highlights are on show in Stedelijk Musem CS, where the museum is temporarily housed near Centraal Station (CS) due to renovations and expansion of its neo-Renaissance home (1895) on the Museumplein. The museum website gives details on the changing exhibitions and events.

The Stedelijk's diverse and formidable collection of modern art and design includes works by Matisse, Mondriaan, Klee, Kandinsky and Keinholz as well as masterpieces by Van Gogh, Picasso, Cézanne, Monet and Chagall. When the Stedelijk Museum opened its doors in 1895 it contained a personal collection bequeathed by Sophia de Bruyn consisting of antiques, coins, jewels, timepieces and silver, along with period rooms from demolished canal houses. It became the National Museum for Modern Art in 1938 and much of the collection focuses on progressive post-war movements. More than 25,000 paintings, drawings, sculptures, photographs, rare posters and graphics comprise the Stedelijk's fascinating acquisitions.

In 1945 museum director Willem Sandberg began collecting works from CoBrA, Expressionism and De Stijl movements. The collection has since grown to include the Malevich collection, works by numerous American artists, Arte Povera, the Young Italians and Minimalists, the Lucebert collection, Mondriaan, among others. Since 1980 there is a special room for video art.

✚ **121 B2**

✉ **Stedelijk Museum CS**
Oosterdokskade 5 (2nd and 3rd floor Post CS building)

☎ 020 573 2911

🌐 **www.stedelijk.nl**

🕐 Daily 10–6; 5 Dec, 24 Dec and 31 Dec 10–5; closed 1 Jan

✋ Expensive

🚋 Tram: 1, 2, 4, 5, 6, 9, 13, 16, 17, 24, 25

Above: A colourful visitor admires a monochrome exhibit in the Stedelijk Museum; **right:** Modern metal sculpture in the Stedelijk garden

Werf 't Kromhout Museum

One of the city's few remaining shipyards that is still in operation, Werf 't Kromhout Museum is also one of the oldest; ships were built here as early as 1757. What makes 't Kromhout unique is the combination of an industrial monument, an operating shipyard and a museum. Opened in 1973, the museum documents the history of the Eastern Docklands and Amsterdam's shipbuilding industry.

Nowadays, the main activities at the shipyard are restoration and repairs of all types of vessels, both historic and modern.

Some of the framed engravings on display here depict Nieuwe Vaart as a busy artery of floating repair platforms and ships at anchor, revealing that the docks are not really active commercially any more. There are plans to install a permanent exhibition that would show the full picture of shipbuilding and the people who lived and worked here. Currently, the museum is the only way to get a glimpse into the Golden Age of Amsterdam's sea voyages.

In the 17th century the flourishing VOC (Vereenigde Oostindische Compagnie) and the Admiralty were able to establish a shipbuilding industry on a much larger scale than before and chose the eastern docks to set the industry going. Over time small private shipyards were founded on the islands – around 30 – though they were not capable of building sea-going vessels. Related industrial activities such as sawmills, rope-walks, smithies and so on took place on the islands.

Until about 1880 this was the leading centre of the shipbuilding industry with wood as the most used material. The name of the shipyard is traced back to one Doede Jansen Kromhout who in 1757 first started a shipyard under the name 't Kromhout meaning a "knee-timber", in clear reference to the wooden ships that were then constructed here.

With the development of the steam engine and the introduction of iron as a building material, new production processes and working skills were necessary in order to stay in business.

Many smaller yards stopped production altogether. In 1899 a part of the yard was rearranged for the construction of steam engines and boilers, and a complete machine shop and an enlarged forge was added. In 1968 the Kromhout Engine was taken over by Werkspoor and the name "Kromhout" became history.

What makes 't Kromhout unique is the combination of an industrial monument, an operating shipyard and a museum. The museum has a fine collection of ancient shipbuilding tools, steam engines and internal combustion engines including the Kromhout engines.

✚ **121 C3**

✉ **Werf 't Kromhout Museum**
Hoogte Kadijk 147

☎ 020 627 6777

🌐 www.machinekamer.nl

🕐 Tue 10–3

💷 Inexpensive

🚌 22, 32, 71,
Wittenburgergracht stop

Windmill De Gooyer & Amsterdam Windmills

The 18th-century windmill De Gooyer is the easiest to find in the city and was built to grind corn. When another building constructed nearby blocked the wind, the windmill was taken apart piece by piece in 1814 and rebuilt on top of the old water pumping station to the east.

If there is sufficient wind, the sails still turn on the first Saturday of the month. Part of the mill is a tiny brewery Brouwerij 't IJ and Proeflokaal (café and tasting room) for their special IJ beer. The terrace is also popular with locals.

Amsterdam was once dotted with windmills, used for pumping water and for grinding corn, mustard, wheat and paint. There are nine windmills in the city environs. For descriptions visit www.simplyamsterdam.nl/amsterdam_windmills.

Another interesting mill is Molen Van Sloten – Sloten Windmill, Akersluis 10, (1847), Amsterdam West (tel: 020 669 0412; open: daily 10–4:30); www.molenvansloten.nl.

Other windmills you might come across (all closed to the public) include:

1100 Roe – Herman Bonpad 6, (1674) Amsterdam West, Osdorp

1200 Roe – Haarlemmerweg 701, (1632) Amsterdam West

De Bloem – Haarlemmerweg 465, (1878) Amsterdam West, Harbour area

De Hoop – Overtoom 430

De Admiraal – Noordhollandschkanaaldijk 21, (1792) Amsterdam North

Gaaspermolen – Lange Stammerdijk 20

Riekermolen – De Borcht 10, (1636), Amsterdam South.

Buitenveldert, also known as De Rieker, is another windmill located on the Amstel river, just outside of town, and was designed to drain the polders (reclaimed low-lying land). It was often sketched by Rembrandt.

Below: Kameleon restaurant under the windmill at Zeeburgerstraat

+ **121 D4**

✉ **Windmill De Gooyer & Amsterdam Windmills**
Funenkade 5

🕐 Windmill closed to public; Brewery Wed–Sun 3–8

✋ Free

🚌 22, 32, 71, Wittenburgergracht stop

Further Afield

Not too far from Amsterdam are places that will give you an even better idea of what life in the Netherlands is all about. Take a stroll in the market squares and quaint streets along charming canals with picturesque landscapes. There are cheese markets, wooden shoes, Delft blue porcelain and much more that's "typically Dutch" in both indoor and open-air museums. See working windmills and craftspeople plying their trades. In season, take a trip through the famous bulb fields, ablaze with colour, or visit the all-year-round flower auction. A vintage tram ride, a flight in a historic aeroplane and boat trips are all possible. Or enjoy a day at the beach, the Ajax football ArenA or shop at the largest multicultural market in Europe.

Alkmaar Cheese Market

Alkmaar is a lovely Old Dutch town with drawbridges over canals, boat tours, a beautiful town hall, patrician houses and picturesque shopping streets in its old centre. The weekly Kaasmarkt, or Cheese Market is popular and well worth the trip.

On Fridays the porters are all dressed in spotless white, with lacquered straw hats. Using leather shoulder slings they carry their wooden trays loaded with up to 80 cannon-ball-sized cheeses weighing around 160kg (330 pounds). The cheese goes to the Waag, a chapel converted into a weighing house in 1582. Inside is Het Hollands Kaasmuseum, (Waagplein 2; tel: (072) 511 4284; www. kaasmuseum.nl; open: Apr–Oct Mon–Thu and Sat 10–4, Fri 9–4) which is all about cheese.

The carillons play on Fridays from 11am to noon (in season) and on Thursdays from 6:30pm–7:30pm and Saturdays noon–1pm.

One block away is Biermuseum De Boom (Houttil 1; tel: 072 511 3801; www.biermuseum.nl; open: Apr–Oct). In this 17th-century brewery you can see how beer is made and taste some of the 90 Dutch varieties. Also of interest is St Laurens Church (Koorstraat 2; tel: 072 514 0707; www.grotekerk-alkmaar.nl; open: Jun–Sep, Tue–Sun 10–5).

Other places to visit are The Hof van Sonoy, Gedempte Nieuwesloot, a former convent; the Huis van Achten (House of Eight) and Hofje van Splinter, an almshouse. The 16th-century Town Hall may be visited on weekdays. Visit the Stedelijk Museum (Canadaplein 1; tel: 072 548 97 89; www. stedelijkmuseumalkmaar. nl; open: Tue–Fri 10–5, Sat–Sun 1–5) for Alkmaar history and a collection of antique toys.

📧 **Alkmaar Cheese Market**
VVV Waagplein 2

☎ 072 548 8888

🌐 **www.alkmaar.nl**

🕐 May–Sep, Fri 10–noon

✋ Free

🚉 Alkmaar

Above: A cheese shop, with a fine selection of cheeses displayed all around

Aalsmeer Flower Auction

The Aalsmeer Flower Auction is an impressive sight. It's the centre of the world's flower industry and the largest flower market in the Netherlands, accounting for 55 per cent of the country's sales. Annually 3.5 billion flowers and 400 million potted plant are sold at this auction alone. The building is the size of 200 football pitches. Some 20 million flowers and 2 million plants are auctioned each day and more than €6.5 million change hands daily.

This trip is for the early riser as you should be in Aalsmeer before 8:30am to take full advantage of the flower auction – it closes when the day's supply of flowers runs out. A catwalk has been constructed over the frenetic auction floor so visitors can see every aspect of the sales process, explained in six languages.

Time is of the essence, and the auction's 1,800 employees quickly wheel in flowers for auction, and out again as soon as they have been sold for rapid transit to their ultimate destination.

A dial by the auctioneer shows the falling prices from 100 to 1. The hand sweeps round, stopping when the price reaches what bidders are willing to spend. The most popular flower sold is the rose, followed by chrysanthemums, tulips and lilies. It's a colourful sight, with Mondays being the busiest day of the week, especially during late spring and early summer. Most of the flowers and plants are destined for European florists and other global customers. For flower parades see www.bloemencorso-bollenstreek.nl and www.bloemencorsoaalsmeer.nl.

Above: Tulips, wrapped and ready for sale, at Aalsmeer

✉ **Aalsmeer Flower Auction**
Bloemenveiling Aalsmeer
Legmeerdijk 313

☎ 029 739 3939

🌐 **www.vba-aalsmeer.com**

🕐 Mon–Fri 7–11

💰 Inexpensive

🚌 172 from Centraal Station

Amsterdam ArenA Stadium

Amsterdam ArenA was the world's first stadium with an underground passageway and the first in Europe with a retractable roof. The legendary Ajax football club has won the national championship 27 times and 25 prestigious international prizes, placing the club among the best in Europe. The multifunctional stadium was built in 1996 and is open for one-hour guided tours. Football fans cheer on the players in Ajax's 17 First Division games, and the stadium also hosts European Cup matches, KNVB international matches, cup and friendly fixtures. It is also home to the American football team, the Amsterdam Admirals. The spectacular venue is also used for pop concerts, theatre performances and special events, playing to capacity crowds with more than 51,600 seats. The stadium boasts state-of-the-art technology and 302 closed-circuit TVs. It has a surface area of 35,000sq m (41,860 square feet).

The World of Ajax Museum

The World of Ajax Museum is all about the club's 100-year-old history and is located here in the stadium. Visitors can enjoy a wealth of exhibits from the club's eventful history, including photographs, historical documents and trophies and television images. Personal possessions of legendary Ajax players are also on display.

Close by on the ArenA Boulevard is Living Tomorrow, the eye-catching house and office of the future (tel: 020 20 30 400, for advance reservations for 90-min tour; www.livingtomorrow.nl).

Amsterdam ArenA Stadium

✉ **Amsterdam ArenA Stadium**
Arena Boulevard 29, Amsterdam ZO

☎ 020 311 1336

🌐 **www.amsterdamarena.nl**

🕐 Guided tours Apr–Sep, daily 11–6; Oct–Mar 11–4:30; no tours during events

✋ Expensive

🚇 50–54 Station Bijlmer ArenA stop

The World of Ajax Museum

✉ **The World of Ajax Museum**

☎ 020 311 1444

🌐 **www.ajax.nl**

🕐 Daily 10–5:30

✋ Moderate

Above: The grand ArenA Football Stadium

Aviodrome (Air Museum)

The Dutch National Aviation Theme Park and Museum Aviodrome has an impressively large collection of historic planes, and is an exciting aviation park. Interactive hands-on expositions bring aviation history back to life, and show the development of the history of air transportation from the early years.

Authentic Dutch and foreign aircraft are presented in beautiful displays that, together with many visual and sound effects, provide the right period atmosphere to document the first attempts at powered flight. Some of the planes may be boarded for closer inspection. The excitement of flying a jet fighter can be experienced first hand via the flight simulator.

For real thrills, actual flights may be booked on historic aircraft such as the Fokker F27 "Friendship", built in 1958, or a vintage Catalina PH-PBY seaplane from 1941. For those with a strong stomach, the pilot can loop the loop and roll you around in a Fokker S11 "Instructor", used as a teaching plane in the 1950s. You may also take flight in the Russian Antonov An-2, the largest single engine biplane in the world, developed in 1947. Other airborne options include aerial views from a Cessna sports plane, a short helicopter flight in a Robinson R44 or an exciting hot-air balloon trip. A 250-seat movie theatre offers spectacular viewing of wide-screen aviation films. Outside in the T-2 hangar, the last flying DC-2 in the world, the Douglas DC-2 "Uiver", can be seen.

Above: One of the many exhibits in the Aviodrome

⌧ **Aviodrome**
Nationaal Luchtvaart-Themapark Aviodrome
Pelikaanweg 50
Lelystad Airport (EHLE)

☎ 0900 284 6376

🌐 www.aviodrome.nl

🕐 Tue–Sun 10–5; closed 1 Jan and 25 Dec

✋ Expensive

🚌 Connexxion 148 from Lelystad to Vliegveld, Eendeweg stop

🚊 To Lelystad

Beverwijkse Bazaar

Beverwijk is best known for its Beverwijkse Bazaar, a place where cultures meet. Billed as Europe's largest indoor market, it offers visitors an unparalleled shopping and culinary adventure with fantastic bargains on enticing goods from around the globe.

Originally known as the "Zwarte" Markt (Black Market), it began in 1980 with 500 stalls and has since grown to 2,500 stalls and shopping units. In 1982, it was joined by the Oosterse Markt (Oriental Market). In 1993, the Grand Bazaar (Eastern Market) opened its doors. The Computer-markt (Computer Market) and the Vlooienmarkt (Flea Market) arrived in 1994. Each of the halls in the massive market have their own unique culture, atmosphere and interesting goods to see, taste and smell.

The huge range of goods on offer makes it almost impossible to see and experience everything in just one day. Apart from clothing, sportswear, perfumes, cosmetics, carpets and household goods, the bazaar is also known for its wide range of traditional and exotic fruits and vegetables. For visitors the market offers a feast for the eyes and for the palate, with delicious drinks, meals and snacks in its 55 multi-cultural restaurants. From May to September there is also a Kofferbakmarkt (car boot sale) where anyone can sell second-hand goods. In April 2007 the new Chinatown market opened, with 180 stores, restaurants, the largest oriental supermarket in the country and China Club, with karaoke, live music and shows (open: Wed–Sun 10–10; www.chinatown holland.nl). There's something for everyone's taste and budget here.

Above: Items in the Flea Market at Beverwijkse Bazaar

✉ **Beverwijkse Bazaar**
  Montageweg 35

☎ 025 126 2666

🌐 **www.debazaar.nl**

🕐 Sat–Sun 8:30–6

🚉 To Beverwijk

🚌 Beverwijk-Oost

Delft

Delft is known for its typical blue-and-white glazed pottery. Splendid Gothic and Renaissance houses lining tree-shaded canals easily make you think that you have been transported to another period in time. The picturesque town founded in 1075 is best seen by taking a horse-drawn tram, a canal tour or by walking away from the busy market square to explore the narrow, residential streets with elegant historic buildings.

As early as the 1300s, Delft was a prosperous town with 200 breweries, but increasing pollution caused many breweries to close. In the 17th century, Dutch East India Company traders began importing blue-and-white porcelain from China. Demand grew so quickly that Delft craftsmen began imitating the designs. Some 30 factories were producing Delftware in the vacant brewery buildings, though, only three remain today. The most famous and best known is De Porceleyne Fles (The Royal Delftware Factory, 1635; Rotterdamseweg 196; tel: 015 251 2030;

www.royaldelft.com; open: Tue–Sun 9–5).

Other attractions include Vermeercentrum (Voldersgracht 21; tel: 015 213 8588; www.vermeerdelft.nl), with four floors honouring master painter Vermeer, Nieuwe Kerk, where William the Silent is buried in a black-and-white marble sarcophagus (Markt 80; tel: 015 212 3025; www.nieuwekerk-delft.nl), the attractive Markt (Market Square), the Waag (Weigh House) and the Boterhuis (1765) behind the town hall, with an elegant façade.

Also visit the Vleeshal and Vishal on the Voldersgracht, Het Prinsenhof (Sint

Agathaplein 1; tel: 015 260 2358; www.prinsenhof-delft.nl), Oude Kerk (1246), Heiligegeest Kerkhof, Museum Lambert and the Leger Museum (Dutch Army Museum).

Above: An artist applying the blue decoration to a piece of Delftware

✉ **Delft**
Tourist Information Point,
Hippolytusbuurt 4

☎ 015 215 4051

🌐 **www.delft.com**

🚌 To Delft

Den Haag

Den Haag (The Hague) has been the seat of government and diplomacy since the 13th century, although Amsterdam is the official capital of the Netherlands. It is the location of the Dutch Parliament and cabinet offices, and is where the Queen lives and works. It is considered an international city of peace and diplomacy.

The Hague's centre is gracious and subdued. Its tree-lined avenues, lovely shopping streets and stylish traditional architecture give it a grace and serenity that sets it apart. Theatre, concerts, dance and a wide variety of restaurants are all excellent and worth sampling. The Hague also has wonderful museums, seaside resorts and 26 parks. Also, there are numerous stately government buildings, embassies, and international organisations such as the International Court of Justice have their headquarters here.

Highlights include the seat of government, Het Binnenhof, between Hofweg and Korte Vijverberg, the Mauritshuis collection of Old Masters and Vermeer (Korte Vijverberg 8; tel:070 302 3456; www.mauritshuis. nl) next door and the Hague Historical Museum (Korte Vijverberg 7; tel: 070 364 6940). Visit the 13th-century Grote Kerk (Rond de Grote Kerk 12; tel: 070 302 8630; www.grotekerkdenhaag. nl), and the Old Town Hall, built in 1565, behind the church. The Peace Palace, Vredespaleis (Carnegieplein 2; tel: 070 302 4137; www.vredespaleis.nl) a magnificent building is a must-see. To see Holland in miniature head to Maudourodam (George Maduroplein 1; tel: 070 416 2400; www.madurodam. nl). Gemeentemusem Den Haag (Stadhouderslaan 41; tel: 070 338 1111) houses a city art collection and Escher in het Paleis (tel: 070 427 7730; www. escherinhetpaleis.nl) has graphics by M C Escher.

✉ **Den Haag**
VVV, Hofweg 1

☎ 0900 340 3505

💻 **www.denhaag.com**

🕐 Visitor Centre Mon–Fri 10–6, Sat 10–5, Sun noon–5

🚉 Den Haag Centraal Station

Above: Den Haag Vredespaleis or the Peace Palace

Edam

Those red, round balls of cheese with their distinctive flavour are produced here and bear the town's name, Edam. In former times the city had 33 shipyards and Edam rivalled Amsterdam, Hoorn and Enkhuizen as a centre of commerce. When the harbour silted up, those prosperous days ended.

The Raadhuis van Edam (Town Hall) on Damplein was built in 1737, and has a beautiful Council Chamber, a magnificent wedding room, antique furniture, hand-painted wallpaper and sand on the floor. It also sponsors temporary exhibits. The richness of the Golden Age of the 17th-century is evident in Edam, making for an interesting and delightfully picturesque town. Between 1778 and 1922, Edam was the marketplace for local cheese producing farmers.

Other highlights include Edams Museum on Damplein 8 (tel: 0299 37 26 44; www.edamsmuseum.nl) in Edam's oldest brick building (1530),once the home of a merchant family; it became a museum in 1895, displaying the history of Edam, and the Captain's House opposite the town hall, which has paintings of regional folktale characters. The Weigh House (1778) on Kaaswaag, Jan Nieuwenhuizenplein 5 (tel: 029 937 2842; open: daily Apr–Sep) still sells cheese. In summer the re-enacted cheese market takes place on Wednesdays from 10:30am to 12:30pm (general market every Wed). Close to the Kaaswaag is the 15th-century Grote Kerk, or St Nicholas Church (Kerkstraat; open: Easter–Sep 2–4:30), with its beautiful choir screen and stained glass windows (1606–1624). Across the canal, the 16th-century Proveniershuis was formerly the home of the Beguine community.

Above: Edam is famous for its cheese

- ✉ **Edam**
  VVV, Damplein 1
- ☎ 029 931 5125
- 🌐 www.vvv-edam.nl
- 🚌 110, 112, 114, 116

Electris chetram museum – Amsterdamse Bos

In this museum you can experience travel in times past during an hour-and-a-half journey in a vintage electric tram, moving along the tracks, rather than looking at displays in exhibition halls. By stepping on board, visitors can truly appreciate what it was like to ride in these trams during the summer months, with fresh air wafting through the open windows and doors.

The vintage trams were all built from 1904 to 1954 and were in service in several European cities, such as Amsterdam, Rotterdam,

The Hague, Groningen, Vienna, Graz and Prague. Though now absent from the streets, they have not been forgotten and have been faithfully restored. In the beautifully renovated former Haarlemmermeer station hall (1915) there is a small exhibition area and souvenir shop. From the rear of the station, vintage trams depart for the village of Amstelveen and Bovenkerk. A tram ride can be enjoyed during the operating season (between Easter and the end of October) on Sundays, and also on Wednesdays in July and August, as well as during special events. The tramway museum is run entirely by volunteers.

Refreshments may be enjoyed in the delightful café-restaurant Prins H inside the station building. The trams run along former railway tracks bordering the Amsterdamse Bos (Amsterdam Forest) with its natural beauty. This is the largest recreational area in Amsterdam.

Several attractions in the forest can easily be reached by foot from tram stops, such as Boerderij Meerzicht (Pancake house in the Amsterdam forest), located at Koenenkade 56 (tel: 020 679 2744).

Above: Canoeing in the canal through the Bos

✉ **Electris chetram museum – Amsterdamse Bos**
Amstelveenseweg 264

☎ 020 673 7538

🌐 **www.museumtramlijn.org
www.museumtram.nl**

🕐 Easter–Oct 10:30–5:40

🎟 Free; donations welcome

🚌 145, 170, 172, 370

Gouda

Known internationally for the cheese which bears its name, the Gouda area produces about 60 per cent of all Dutch cheese. Every Thursday from mid-June to the end of August the old-fashioned cheese market is re-enacted for the benefit of tourists.

Gouda has the largest market square in the Netherlands, and sitting in the middle of it is the oldest free-standing Gothic town hall in the country, dating from 1450 (Markt 1).

Also on the square is the Kaas Waag or Weigh House, built in 1668. Upstairs in the Weigh House is the Cheese Museum (tel: 018 252 9996). The city was once one of Europe's premier makers of pottery and long white clay pipes, which can be seen in De Moriaan National Pharmaceutical Museum (Westhaven 29; tel: 018 233 1000). It was also a centre for candle-making, and its Gouda kaarsen are

the longest-burning candles. In December the city is traditionally lit by candlelight. Gouda stroopwafels, caramel-filled wafers, are also considered Holland's very best.

Most impressive of the attractions is the marvellous 16th-century collection of 70 stained-glass windows in St Janskerk, depicting Dutch history and events in the Bible, on sunny days they can be admired in their best light (tel: 018 251 2684). The Catharina Gasthuis Museum (1542), Achter de Kerk 14, behind the Church (tel: 018 233 1000; open: Wed–Sun noon–5) and a working flour windmill De Roode Leeuw

(the Red Lion), Vest 65 (tel: 018 252 2041) are the other places of note.

Above: The old Stadthuis town hall, Gouda

✉ **Gouda**
VVV, Markt 27

☎ 018 251 1300

🌐 **www.vvvgouda.nl**

🕐 Visitor Centre
Mon 1–5:30, Tue–Fri 9:30–5:30, Sat 10–4

🚉 To Gouda

Haarlem

Haarlem is more than 900 years old and filled with historic buildings, unique shops and deliciously diverse restaurants. The original hunting lodge (1250) became the ornately gabled town hall in the 14th century. Sights are all close together and the VVV has a tour map that makes exploring easy and delightful. The town's atmosphere is inviting and there is plenty to captivate the visitor.

Most historic buildings date from the 17th century, Haarlem's greatest period of prosperity. The secret gardens of Haarlem or "Haarlemse Hofjes" are located in 22 secluded courtyards in the centre.

⊠ **Haarlem**
VVV, Stationsplein 1

☎ 0900 616 1600

🌐 **www.haarlem.nl**
**www.haarlemshuffle.
com**

🕐 Visitor Centre Apr–Sep, Mon–Fri 9–5:30, Sat 10–4; Oct–Mar, Mon–Fri 9:30–5, Sat 10–3

🚉 To Haarlem

Highlights of the town include the Grote Markt Square and the Grotekerk St Bavo (built 1390–1520), with its famous Muller organ which Mozart once played (tel: 023 553 2040; www. bavo.nl). Next door is the Vleeshal (1602) with its highly ornamented step-gables. The Archeologisch Museum (Grote Markt 18; tel: 023 542 0888) is in the basement. Also visit De Hallon (Grote Markt 16; tel: 023 511 5775) for modern art; Verweyhal by the artist Kees Verwey (www.dehallen. com); the Hoofdwacht (Guard House) on the northeast corner; Corrie ten Boom House – The Hiding Place (Barteljorisstraat 19, north of the Grote Markt; tel: 023 531 0823;

www.corrietenboom. com). The Frans Hals Museum (Groot Heiligland 62, tel: 023 511 5775; www.franshalsmuseum. nl) is a former almshouse and orphanage. It shows paintings by Frans Hals and other Dutch masters. Also on this attractive street are 17th-century Gasthuisjes and the Historisch Museum Zuid-Kennemerland (Groot Heiligland 47; tel: 023 542 2427; www. historischmuseumhaarlem.nl) telling the history of Haarlem and Teylers Museum (Spaarne 16; tel: 023 516 0960; www.teylersmuseum. nl) which houses its collection in the country's oldest museum (1778).

Above: Historic buildings in Haarlem

Hoorn

Hoorn was once a rich, internationally known town and a base of the Dutch East India trading company. Founded in the 14th century on the site of a natural harbour, seafaring adventurers embarked from the attractive Binnenhaven and returned with exotic goods, bringing its citizens wealth and power during the 17th century. It's an ideal town to explore, with interesting historical landmarks and many charming shops.

The Westfries Museum, in the former State Council building (1632) with a baroque façade is located in the red-brick town square, the most picturesque part of Hoorn (Rode Steen 1; tel: 022 928 0028; www.wfm. nl). Opposite is the Waag, or Weigh House (1609), now a restaurant. From the square, Kerkstraat leads to the Grote Kerk. Facing it is St Jans Gasthuis, one of the city's most attractive buildings, a former hospital (1563). On Nieuwstraat is the Statenpoort (1613) with twin stepped gables. Other highlights are: Museum Van De Twintigste Eeuw (Museum of the 20th century) at Bierkade 4 (tel: 022 921 4001) with displays of household items and artefacts. A scale model shows Hoorn as it was in 1650. In the pleasant harbour area, now primarily for leisure yachts, is Oosterkerk, Grote Oost with its 17th-century façade, formerly the seamen's family church. The romantic Hoofdtoren on Veermanskade is a defence tower from 1532. Museumstoomtram Hoorn-Medemblik (Van Dedemstraat 8; tel: 022 921 4862) offers old-fashioned steam locomotive rides between Hoorn and Medemblik in the summer.

Above: Attractive Hoorn harbour

✉ **Hoorn**
VVV-ANWB Veemarkt 4

☎ 072 511 4284 / 0900 403 1055

🌐 **www.vvvhoorn.nl**

🚊 To Hoorn

Keukenhof Gardens

Open from the end of March to the end of May, the Keukenhof or "kitchen garden" is arguably the most beautiful flower park in the world, and also one of most photographed places. More than 7 million flowers bloom here. In autumn, more than 6 million bulbs are planted in this 28ha (70-acre) park, resulting in a brilliant springtime riot of colour.

The dazzling display of colours and fragrances is a delight indeed. Every year the plantings are different, so the displays are always new. Early in the season, crocuses, hyacinths, narcissi, azaleas and trees blossom, and then come the tulips in all their glorious hues. Large pavilions, protected from rain and wind, with a complete range of flowers, elaborate cut flower arrangements, more than 600 varieties of tulips, daffodils and other spring plants in garden layouts, are featured in changing displays.

There are sculptures throughout the park, as well as model gardens, self-service restaurants, flower shops and a working windmill. Originally, the park closed for the season in May when the bulbs were dug up and the ground prepared for next year. In 1999 (its 50th anniversary), Keukenhof organised its first Zomerhof, from mid-August to mid-September, now a permanent feature. It covers about 7ha (17 acres) and includes bulbs and tuberous plants such as lilies and begonias, as well as roses and perennials. Many growers are represented at Keukenhof, who will ship bulbs abroad. The park receives more than 900,000 visitors in the few weeks it is open every year. Early in the day is less crowded.

- ✉ **Keukenhof Gardens**
  Stationsweg 166 a

- ☎ 025 246 5555

- 🌐 **www.keukenhof.nl**

- 🕐 Late Mar to mid-May daily 8–7:30; Zomerfest mid-Aug to mid-Sep 9–6

- ✋ Expensive

- 🚌 54 Leiden stop; 50, 51 Haarlem stop

Above: Flowers in the Keukenhof Gardens

Leiden

Leiden is a city with a rich history, the nation's oldest university, picturesque canals and 12 museums, containing internationally renowned, unique and priceless collections. It is also where Rembrandt was born and developed his painting skills and botanists cultivated the first Dutch tulips. By 1644 its large textile industry had made it the second largest city in the country.

Some of the greatest Dutch artists were born here, including Rembrandt and Jan Steen. The Pilgrims lived here for 11 years before sailing to America. Leiden University, the first established in the Netherlands (1575), is a world-famous centre of science and gives the city its convivial and lively "student town" atmosphere. There is a good selection of shops and restaurants and a large general market is held on Wednesdays and Saturdays.

Highlights include: Pieterskerk, Pieterskerkhof 1a; tel: 071 512 4319; www.pieterskerk.com.

Rijksmuseum Van Oudheden – National Museum of Antiquities, Rapenburg 28; tel: 071 516 3163; www.rmo.nl.

Molenmuseum De Valk – Windmill Museum, 2e Binnenvestgracht; tel: 071 516 5353.

Rijksmuseum Voor Volkenkunde – National Museum of Ethnology , Steenstraat 1; tel: 071 516 8800; www.rmv.nl.

Stedelijk Museum de Lakenhal, Oudesingel 28-32; tel: 071 516 5360; www.lakenhal.nl for textile industry and art.

Museum Boerhaave – Museum for the History of Science, Lange St Agnietenstraat 10; tel: 071 521 4224; www.museumboerhaave.nl.

Hortus Botanicus – Leiden University Botanical Gardens; tel: 071 527 7249.

Naturalis – National Museum of Natural History,

Darwinweg 2, tel: 071 568 7600; www.naturalis.nl, with fossils, dinosaurs, geology; Leiden American Pilgrim Museum, Beschuitsteeg 9, tel: 071 512 2413.

Above: A riot of colour in Leiden tulip fields

✉ **Leiden**
VVV, Stationsweg 2D

☎ 071 516 1211

ᵂᵂᵂ **www.hollandrijnland.nl**

◔ Visitor Centre
Apr–Aug, Mon 11–5:30, Tue–Fri 9:30–5:30, Sat 10–4:30, Sun 11–3; closed Sun Sep–Jul

🚆 NS from Amsterdam

Volendam and Marken

These former fishing villages are among the most charming in the Netherlands. Inhabited since the 13th century, Volendam is a Roman Catholic town and Marken is Protestant. With the draining of the Zuiderzee for the Afsluitdijk and the demise of the local fishing industry, the towns turned to tourism.

Volendam is larger than Marken, but both have retained some of their traditional feel in spite of tourist influx. One of the attractions is seeing some of the locals dressed in traditional costumes. The hotel-restaurant Spaander (Haven 15–19; tel: 029 936 3595) has a collection of more than 100 paintings from 19th-century artists who came here to paint. The Volendams Museum (Zeestraat 41; tel: 029 936 9258; www.volendams-museum.com; open: mid-Mar to mid-Oct daily 10–5) displays traditional costumes, old photographs, paintings, four model interiors of Zuiderzee homes and a collection of 11 million cigar bands. From May to June there's a weekly fish auction on the Haven every morning from Monday to Friday. Many visitors are pictured while dressed in the traditional Dutch costumes.

Marken has old-world charm with its traditional green-and-white painted gabled houses built on piles.

Have a look at Het Marker Museum (Kerkbuurt 44–47; tel: 029 960 1904; open: Easter–Oct, Mon–Sat 10–5, Sun noon–4) located in four former fishermen's homes, with the original interiors, showing Marken life and history. See how typical Dutch wooden clogs are made at Marker Klompenmakerij (Kets 50; tel: 029 960 1630; open: all year).

Above: A view of Volendam waterfront

✉ **Volendam and Marken**
VVV Zeestraat 37

☎ 029 936 3747

🌐 **www.vvv-volendam.nl**

🕐 Visitor Centre 18 Mar–Oct, Mon–Sat 10–5; Nov–17 Mar, Mon–Sat 10–3

🚌 From Arriva Station

Zaanse Schans

For a fascinating trip back in time with definite Dutch ambience, explore Zaanse Schans, an Old Dutch village. It is a living museum of homes, historic buildings and windmills, dating from the 17th to the 19th centuries. The houses are actually inhabited by private citizens, which makes them a living attraction with an active history.

These characteristic wooden houses and mills were all transported from the neighbouring area by boat and were reconstructed here in the 1960s as a monument to village life. In one windmill you can buy excellent Zaanse mustard which has been milled on the spot, and buy groceries in the very first Albert Heijn supermarket. The Visitor Centre provides a brochure listing all the attractions and a map. At one time 600 windmills dominated the skyline; today only 12 remain. The carefully restored windmills are operated by the inhabitants and used for grinding flour, making mustard, grinding pigments for paint, as well as the last working oil mill and mills for generating power and for sawing logs into building timber. The Zaans Museum (Schansend 7; tel: 075 616 2862; www. zaansmuseum.nl) offers an overview of the region's history. Visit Zaanse Schans Klompenmakerij (Kraaiennest 4; tel: 075 617 7121; www. woodenshoeworkshop.nl), a wooden clog workshop and De Tinkoepel (Kalverringdijk 1; tel: 075 617 6204; www. tinkoepel.nl) an 18th-century teahouse. Also see the windmill museum at Koog aan de Zaan, the Molenmuseum (Museumlaan 18; tel: 075 621 5148; www.zaansemolen.nl). At Zaandijk, admire Zaanse objects and 17th- and 18th-century clothing at the Zaans Historisch Museum (Lagedijk 80; tel: 075 621 7626).

Below: Two of the twelve windmills at Zaanse Schans

✉ **Zaanse Schans**
Schansend 1
Zaandam

☎ 075 616 8218

🌐 **www.zaanseschans.nl**

🕒 Visitor Centre daily 9–5 (some attractions closed during the week in winter)

🚉 To Aalkmaar, Koog aan Dijk

Zandvoort Beach

Once a sleepy fishing village dating from 1100, Zandvoort is now one of the country's major beach resorts and has plenty to offer in by way of recreation, shopping, restaurants and natural beauty with its miles of sandy beaches. A short trip from Amsterdam brings you sea breezes and beach fun.

Zandvoort is advantageously located in a natural scenic area with bird habitats, lakes, woods and beaches. In the 19th century tourism started to flourish. The Badhuis (Bathhouse) was built in 1828 and hotels, shops and luxury villas sprang up. The railway connection was completed in 1881 and brought in even more visitors. Fishing still makes up part of its economy, though it relies a lot on tourism. Today, Zandvoort annually welcomes more than 4 million visitors.

There's also a Holland Casino (Badhuisplein 7; tel: 023 574 0574; open: daily 1:30pm–3am), the Zandvoorts Museum (Swaluëstraat 1; tel: 023 57 40 280; open: mid-Apr–Aug, Wed, Sat–Sun noon–4:30) which covers the town's history, with traditional clothing and period rooms. Zandvoort is probably best known for its racetrack, the Circuit Park Zandvoort (Burg van Alphenstraat 108; tel: 023 574 0740), with regularly scheduled motor races. For nature walks in the dunes head to Kennermerduinen Park (Visitor's Centre, Tetterodeweg 27, Overveen; tel: 023 541 1123; open: mid-Apr to mid-Sep, daily 9–4:30). Walk from the Zandvoort railway station along the Boulevard. In high season there is also a beach bus to take you along the beachfront to cafés.

✉ **Zandvoort Beach**
VVV Zandvoort
Schoolplein 1

☎ 023 571 2262

🌐 **www.vvvzk.nl**

🕐 Visitor Centre
Apr–Sep, Mon–Fri 9–4:30, Sat 9–4; Nov–Mar, Mon–Fri 9–12:30, 1:30–4:30

🚆 From Amsterdam to Zandvoort

Above: Zandvoort Beach

Zuiderzeemuseum

The Zuiderzeemuseum takes you back in time to its Buitenmuseum, a reconstructed Old Dutch village on the shores of the Ijsselmeer, (formerly the Zuiderzee). When the Afsluitdijk was built in the 1930s, access to the North Sea was blocked which devastated the local fishing economy.

Some 130 buildings were dismantled piece-by-piece and reassembled along streets and canals of the Zuiderzeemuseum, providing a picture of life from 1880–1932. Craftsmen from all trades are shown demonstrating their work: a blacksmith, a butcher, a baker and you can see fish-smoking, sail-making and net-mending. There is an old schoolhouse and a working steam laundry (1900). Children can play with old-fashioned toys and dress in traditional Dutch costume, complete with wooden clogs.

The Indoor Museum is located in The Peperzolder or Pepper Attic, a historic building that was once the headquarters of the Enkhuizen Chamber of the Dutch East India Company. It has the largest collection of boats in the country and 25,000 objects reflecting seven centuries of Zuiderzee and Ijsselmeer history. Highlights include national costumes in authentic period interiors, Hindeloopen and Zaans painted furniture, farmhouse utensils, ship models, and many nautical objects, such as old-style anchors and fishing nets. A unique fleet of Zuiderzee and inland ships lies moored at the quay. In the covered hall of ships, old vessels may be viewed from a walkway.

Zuiderzeemuseum is entered by museum ferryboat from the car park every 15 minutes. There is a regular shuttle service from the train station jetty to the boat. The Indoor Museum is a 10-minute walk from the station.

Above: The Outdoor Museum

✉ **Zuiderzeemuseum**
Wierdijk 12–22
Enkhuizen

☎ 0228 35 1111

🌐 **www.zuiderzee museum.nl**

🕐 Indoor Museum daily 10–5 (closed Mon Nov–Mar); Outdoor Museum Mar–Oct 10–5

✋ Expensive

🚌 From Centraal Station

Listings

Part of the pleasure of a stay in Amsterdam is finding those charming places to stay, right in the heart of the action in the city centre or in the quieter outlying areas along the canals. Numerous restaurants tempt any palate. There are snack bars, places serving ethnic cuisine to grand establishments and those boasting Michelin stars. Shops range from quirky to sublime, with chic boutiques, major department stores and flea markets. And after the day's sightseeing, there is enough entertainment to suit the most discerning patron of the arts – from clubs, concerts, cinema, comedy and theatre to dance and live gigs.

Accommodation

Fortunately, Amsterdam is an easy city to move around – so wherever you stay, your location is always convenient for most of the sights or a mere tram ride away from the rest. Amsterdam has around 37,760 hotel beds and receives more than 7 million visitors annually. Two-fifths of these beds are in top-range properties, making mid-range and budget accommodation more difficult to find. Hotels or B&Bs along lovely canals in 17th-century mansions, although charming, are more expensive and may prove inconvenient with steep, narrow stairs and no lifts. Elegant canals include Keizersgracht, Singel and Prinsengracht. Downtown areas around the Leidseplein, Dam square and Rembrandtplein are where the action is, but if you want a quieter stay settle for the Vondelpark and the Museum Quarter.

€ under €100
€€ €100–200
€€€ over €200

CENTRAL AMSTERDAM

Agora €
This is a comfortable, centrally located 18th-century canal house furnished with some wonderful antiques.
✉ Singel 462, Grachtengordel
☎ 020 627 2200
🌐 www.hotelagora.nl
🚊 4, 9, 14, 16, 24, 25

Amsterdam €€
Behind its 18th-century façade is a fully modern hotel in the hub of one of the city's busiest tourist streets. The 80 rooms here offer the best facilities and make this hotel a great place to stay.
✉ Damrak 93–94, Centrum
☎ 020 555 0666
🌐 www.hotelamsterdam.nl
🚊 4, 9, 14, 16, 24, 25

Amsterdam House €€
A small hotel, quietly situated beside the Amstel river. There are 16 rooms and most

of them have a lovely view of the river.
✉ 's-Gravenlandseveer 3–4, Centrum
☎ 020 624 6607
🌐 www.amsterdamhouse.com
🚊 4, 9, 14, 16, 24, 25

Crowne Plaza Amsterdam City Centre €€
A centrally located, well-furnished hotel with 270 rooms and a good range of facilities. A roof-top terrace, a swimming pool and gym are some of the features that this hotel offers. The Dutch cuisine in the restaurant De Roode Leeuw is highly recommended.
✉ Nieuwezijds Voorburgwal 5, Centrum
☎ 020 620 0500
🌐 www.amsterdam-citycentre.crowneplaza.com
🚊 4, 9, 14, 16, 24, 25

De l'Europe €€–€€€
This prestigious establishment combines classic old-world charm with belle époque architecture. Situated along the waterfront, this property has 100 rooms with all the modern amenities.
✉ Nieuwe Doelenstraat 2–8, Centrum
☎ 020 531 1777
🌐 www.leurope.nl
🚊 4, 6, 9, 14, 16, 24, 25

Grand Sofitel Demeure Amsterdam €€€
A former royal inn and a City Hall, this 16th-century building is now a luxury hotel with an interesting historical atmosphere. The regal service and classic interiors imbue the place with a touch of royalty.
✉ Oudezijds Voorburgwal 197, Centrum
☎ 020 555 3111
🌐 www.thegrand.nl
🚇 Nieuwmarkt stop

Nova €
This simple hotel is quite centrally located behind the Royal Palace in five beautifully renovated historic buildings. There are 61 rooms available and the members of staff are very friendly and helpful.

✉ Nieuwezijds Voorburgwal 276, Centrum
☎ 020 623 0066
🌐 www.novahotel.nl
🚊 1, 2, 5

Nh Doelen €€
This is the city's oldest hotel and the place where Rembrandt painted his *Night Watch*. The 85 rooms are small yet well-equipped.
✉ Nieuwe Doelenstraat 24, Centrum
☎ 020 554 0600
🌐 www.nh-hotels.com
🚊 4, 9, 14, 16, 24, 25

WESTERN CANALS & JORDAAN

Acacia €
Located in the heart of the lively Jordaan district this is a cheerful, family-run hotel with studio rentals and two houseboats.
✉ Lindengracht 251, Jordaan
☎ 020 622 1460
🌐 www.hotelacacia.nl
🚊 3

Ambassade €€
An elegant B&B located in a 17th-century gabled canal house. The 59 rooms with antique furniture are charming.
✉ Herengracht 341, Grachtengordel
☎ 020 555 0222
🌐 www.ambassade-hotel.nl
🚊 1, 2, 5

Canal House €€
Situated on a beautiful canal, the Keizersgracht, this small family-run hotel is the perfect base from which to explore the city. All the 26 rooms are tastefully decorated in a classic 17th-century style.
✉ Keizersgracht 148, Grachtengordel
☎ 020 622 5182
🌐 www.canalhousehotel.com
🚊 6, 13, 14, 17

Estheréa €€
Warm and inviting family-owned hotel with beautiful views along the canal. The

canalside character gives the place a charming appeal. The service is efficient and the rooms are equipped with all the modern facilities including internet.

✉ Singel 303–309, Grachtengordel
☎ 020 624 5146
🆆 www.estherea.nl
🚌 1, 2, 5

ITC €€
Located in the heart of old Amsterdam, this is a quiet hotel with a lovely garden, located on the beautiful Prinsengracht canal.

✉ Prinsengracht 1051, Grachtengordel
☎ 020 623 0230
🆆 www.itc-hotel.com
🚌 4

Maas €€
A family-run, charming waterfront hotel with 28 rooms, located close to many museums, shops and bars.

✉ Leidsekade 91, Grachtengordel
☎ 020 623 3868
🆆 www.hotelmaas.nl
🚌 1, 2, 5, 6, 7, 10

NH Barbizon Palace €€
A row of gorgeous 17th-century mansions deftly conceals this modern luxury hotel with 274 rooms. Amid the hotel's marble tiles and antique beams, sits the award-winning Vermeer restaurant. The place exudes elegance and sophistication.

✉ Prins Hendrikkade 59–72, Centrum
☎ 020 556 4564
🆆 www.nh-hotels.com
🚉 Centraal Station

NH Grand Hotel Krasnapolsky €€€
The "Kras" as it's known, was built in the 1880s and has belle époque elegance in its public spaces. Its 469 rooms offer all the modern facilities.

✉ Dam 9, Centrum
☎ 020 554 9111
🆆 www.nh-hotels.com
🚌 1, 2, 4, 5, 9, 13, 14, 16, 17, 24, 25

NH Schiller €€
Built in 1912, this art deco hotel is situated in the popular Rembrandtplein with its bars, restaurants and outdoor café terraces.

✉ Rembrandtplein 26, Grachtengordel
☎ 020 554 0700
🆆 www.nh-hotels.com
🚌 4, 9, 14

Prins Hendrik €€
Situated opposite Centraal Station, this newly renovated hotel has a cosy bar and restaurant, as well as stunning views of the Amsterdam skyline.

✉ Prins Hendrikkade 52–57, Centrum
☎ 020 623 7969
🆆 www.hotel-prinshendrik.nl
🚌 All trams to Centraal Station

Prinsenhof €
Quaint and comfortable budget hotel situated on a peaceful canal in a quiet area close to Rembrandtplein with its numerous restaurants, bars and cafés.

✉ Prinsengracht 810, Grachtengordel
☎ 020 623 1772
🆆 www.hotelprinsenhof.com
🚌 4

Pulitzer €€€
Twenty-four 17th-century houses were converted to create this luxurious canalside hotel with an authentic Dutch ambience.

✉ Prinsengracht 315–331, Grachtengordel
☎ 020 523 5235
🆆 www.pulitzer.nl
🚌 6, 13, 14, 17

Seven Bridges €€
Small, exquisite hotel on one of the city's prettiest canals. This friendly hotel offers 11 individually decorated stylish rooms complete with oriental carpets and handcrafted marquetry furniture.

✉ Reguliersgracht 31, Grachtengordel
☎ 020 623 1329
🆆 www.sevenbridgeshotel.nl
🚌 4

Seven One Seven €€€
This luxurious B&B with friendly staff looks more like a home than a boutique hotel. The eight bedrooms are inspired by painters, authors and composers.
✉ Prinsengracht 717, Grachtengordel
☎ 020 427 0717
ⓦ www.717hotel.nl
🚌 1, 2, 5, 6, 7, 10

EASTERN CANALS

Amstel Intercontinental €€€
Amsterdam's most luxurious, exclusive and expensive hotel. Its location on the water and its chic decor make it a most charming place to stay.
✉ Prof Tulpplein 1, Amstel
☎ 020 622 6060
ⓦ www.ihg.com
🚌 6, 7, 10

Best Western Lancaster Hotel €€
Built in 1890, this hotel with 92 rooms has been renovated completely. The relaxing rooms with beige and terracotta colour scheme offer period charm.
✉ Plantage Middenlaan 48
☎ 020 535 6888
ⓦ www.edenhotelgroup.com
🚌 9, 14

Hotel Rembrandt €
Small family-run hotel, with a Rembrandt theme throughout. The 17 rooms feature all the state-of-the-art facilities.
✉ Plantage Middenlaan 17
☎ 020 627 2714
ⓦ www.hotelrembrandt.nl
🚌 9, 14

MUSEUM QUARTER

Amsterdam American €€€
This resplendent art nouveau classic is located on the busy Leidseplein, and is also a favourite spot for drinks and dinner.
✉ Leidsekade 97, Grachtengordel
☎ 020 556 3000
ⓦ www.amsterdamamerican.com
🚌 1, 2, 5, 6, 7, 10

Atlas €€
This attractive art nouveau hotel provides a relaxing stay near Vondelpark. The lively, popular Leidseplein is close by, as are many museums and the top shopping street PC Hooftstraat.
✉ Van Eeghenstraat 64, Oud West
☎ 020 676 6336
ⓦ www.hotelatlas.nl
🚌 2, 3, 12

Bilderberg Garden €€
A relaxing hotel located in a pleasant green suburban area, just a short tram ride from the city centre. It combines international style and luxury with a warm and intimate atmosphere.
✉ Dijsselhofplantsoen 7, Oud Zuid
☎ 020 570 5600
ⓦ www.gardenhotel.nl
🚌 16

EASTERN DOCKLANDS & IJ HARBOUR

Amstel Botel €
A floating boat-hotel (botel) with magnificent views over IJ Harbour and the old docks.
✉ Oosterdokskade 2–4, Oosterdok
☎ 020 626 4247
ⓦ www.amstelbotel.com
🚉 Centraal Station

Arena €
This hotel is situated in a charming former 19th-century orphanage alongside Amsterdam's historical city centre. The facilities include a café, bar, restaurant, club and conference rooms.
✉ 's-Gravesandestraat 51, Oost and Oosterdok
☎ 020 850 2400
ⓦ www.hotelarena.nl
🚌 7, 10

Restaurants

Traditional hearty Dutch food may actually not be easy to find. The trend leans towards lighter "New Dutch" cooking. The selection of tastes and flavours adding their ingredients to the multicultural mix that makes up Amsterdam have certainly spiced up the variety of culinary experiences available in the city. Blending centuries of colonialism, the Dutch developed a taste for exotic cuisines. The most common ethnic dishes are Indonesian and Chinese. An Indonesian *rijsttafel* (rice table) features rice along with some 15 to 30 side dishes of meat, fish, egg and vegetables. There is something to suit everyone's taste in a wide variety of restaurants from around the globe.

€ under €20
€€ €20–40
€€€ over €40

CENTRAL AMSTERDAM

1E Klas €
Café in the former wood panelled first-class waiting rooms at Amsterdam's Centraal Station, located on Platform 2.
✉ Centraal Station, Stationsplein 15
☎ 020 625 0131
🕓 Daily 8:30am–11pm
🚇 Centraal Station

Aneka Rasa €€
This modern restaurant with its airy, tropical ambience serves numerous vegetarian dishes including an all-vegetarian *rijsttafel*.
✉ Warmoesstraat 25–29, Centrum
☎ 020 626 1560
🕓 Daily 5–10:30
🚇 Centraal Station

De Brakke Grond €–€€
Enjoy bountiful portions of Belgian food and a choice of Belgian beers in the Flemish Cultural Centre's atmospheric restaurant or on their spacious terrace.

✉ Nes 43, Centrum
☎ 020 626 0044
🕐 Mon–Thu 11am–1am, Fri–Sat 11am–2am,
Sun noon–1am
🌐 www.brasseriedebrakkegrond.nl
🚌 4, 9, 14, 16, 24, 25

Café Pacifico €
The best and most authentic Mexican
restaurant in town. Tuesday is margarita
night, so it gets very crowded.
✉ Warmoesstraat 31, Centrum
☎ 020 624 2911
🕐 Sun–Thu 5–10:30, Fri–Sat 5–11
🌐 www.cafepacifico.nl
🚉 Centraal Station

Caffé Esprit €
Designer café housed in a glass and
aluminium structure, part of the trendy
clothing boutique next door. Sandwiches,
salads, burgers and bagels are on
the menu.
✉ Spui 10a, Centrum
☎ 020 622 1967
🕐 Mon–Sat 9–6 (also Thu 10–10),
Sun noon–6
🌐 www.caffeesprit.nl
🚌 1, 2, 4, 5, 9, 14, 16, 24, 25

Dorrius €€€
Enjoy rustic Dutch style food with a
sophisticated twist. Traditional fish
delicacies (pike and cod) and tasty cheese
soufflés are very popular.
✉ Crowne Plaza Hotel, Nieuwezijds
Voorburgwal 5, Centrum
☎ 020 420 2224
🕐 Mon–Sat 6–11
🌐 www.dorrius.nl
🚌 1, 2, 5, 13, 17

Dynasty €€€
Sumptuous South East Asian cuisine
served in a sophisticated, richly decorated
garden restaurant.
✉ Reguliersdwarsstraat 30, Grachtengordel
☎ 020 626 8400

🕐 Wed–Mon dinner only
🚌 16, 24, 25

WESTERN CANALS & JORDAAN

Albatros €€–€€€
The daily catch is served in a quaint and
unpretentious, homely atmosphere.
✉ Westerstraat 264, Jordaan
☎ 020 627 9932
🕐 Thu–Tue from 6pm
🚌 3, 10

De Belhamel €€
Continental cuisine is on the menu in this
intimate restaurant, with an art nouveau
interior. There is live classical music and a
superb canal view.
✉ Brouwersgracht 60, Jordaan
☎ 020 622 1095
🕐 Daily lunch noon–4, dinner 6–10
🚌 1, 2, 5, 6, 13, 17

De Blauwe Hollander €
Wholesome and reasonably priced food,
with generous portions.
✉ Leidsekruisstraat 28, Grachtengordel
☎ 020 627 0521
🕐 Daily lunch, dinner
🚌 1, 2, 5, 7, 10

Bloemgracht €€
A modern restaurant in an old canalside
house. A young enthusiastic team offers
creative Mediterranean cooking with
a twist.
✉ Bloemgracht 47, Jordaan
☎ 020 620 2088
🕐 Tue–Thu, Sun6–10, Fri–Sat 6–10:30
🌐 www.restaurantbloemgracht.nl
🚌 12, 14, 17

Bojo €€
Indonesian food with large portions of rice
and noodle dishes, sate, and plenty of
vegetarian choices. Late night dining,
open daily until 2am and at weekends
until 4am.

☒ Lange Leidsedwarsstraat 49–51,
Grachtengordel
☎ 020 622 7434
🕓 Mon–Fri 4pm–2am, Sat–Sun noon–4am
🌐 www.bojo.nl
🚌 1, 2, 5, 7, 10

De Bolhoed €
On the edge of the Jordaan, this trendy restaurant serves vegetarian pâtés, fresh salads and hearty vegan dishes.
☒ Prinsengracht 60–62,
Grachtengordel
☎ 020 626 1803
🕓 Daily lunch noon–5, dinner 5–10
🚌 13, 14, 17

Christophe €€€
Imaginative French gastronomic concoctions in an elegant and charming canalside restaurant.
☒ Leliegracht 46, Jordaan
☎ 020 625 0807
🕓 Tue–Sat 6:30–10:30
🌐 www.restaurantchristophe.nl
🚌 6, 13, 14, 17, 20

Cinema Paradiso €€
A piece of Italy in Amsterdam, this spacious restaurant serves authentic Italian dishes. It uses cheeses imported from Italy, fresh herbs and also has a varied selection of wines.
☒ Westerstraat 184–186, Jordaan
☎ 020 623 7344
🕓 Tue–Sun 6–11
🌐 www.cinemaparadiso.info
🚌 3, 10

The Dylan Restaurant €€€
Classic and contemporary cuisine from East and West, in the elegant Dylan hotel, renowned for its delicious blending of both culinary cultures.
☒ Keizersgracht 384, Grachtengordel
☎ 020 530 2010
🕓 Mon–Sat lunch noon–2, dinner 7–10:30
🚌 1, 2, 5

Gary's Muffins €
Serves delicious fresh, warm, muffins, generously filled bagels and brownies.
☒ Prinsengracht 454, Grachtengordel
☎ 020 420 1452
🕓 Daily lunch, dinner
🚌 1, 2, 5, 13, 17

Gelateria Jordino €
Serves great home-made Italian ice cream and chocolate cake in a bright, friendly atmosphere.
☒ Haarlemmerdijk 25, Centrum
☒ 020 420 3225
🕓 Daily 10–8
🚌 1, 2, 5, 13, 17

Pancake Bakery €
With a choice of some 50 different kinds of pancakes, this is a good place to take the children. Its location in the basement of an old canal house makes it a great draw.
☒ Prinsengracht 191, Grachtengordel
☎ 020 625 1333
🕓 Daily noon–9:30
🌐 www.pancake.nl
🚌 13, 14, 17

Restaurant Bloesem €€
An informal, relaxed restaurant with touches of gold gilt. The two dining areas are interconnected by arches. Choose from meat, game, fish or vegetarian dishes.
☒ Binnen Dommersstraat 13, Jordaan
☎ 020 770 0407
🕓 Sun–Thu 5pm–1am, Fri–Sat 5–2am
🌐 www.restaurantbloesem.nl
🚌 7, 10, 16, 24, 25

Sherpa €
An interesting Nepalese/Tibetan venue, decorated with traditional Himalayan ornaments. Nepalese meals are rather spicy; Tibetan dishes are prepared with noodles and ravioli.
☒ Korte Leidsedwarsstraat 58,
Grachtengordel
☎ 020 623 9495

- Dinner only (lunch in summer)
- www.sherpa-restaurant.nl
- 1, 2, 5, 6, 7, 10

Toscanini €€
Serves delicious Italian dishes.
- Lindengracht 75, Jordaan
- 020 623 2813
- Mon–Sat dinner only
- 3

Van Puffelen €€
Wholesome French-style cooking is served in this classic brown café.
- Prinsengracht 375–377, Grachtengordel
- 020 624 6270
- Mon–Wed 3–11, Thu–Sun noon–11)
- 13, 14, 17, 20

De Vliegende Schotel €–€€
The vegetarian menu at "The Flying Saucer" includes generous portions, filling soups, salads, noodles and *rijsttafel*.
- Nieuwe Leliestraat 162–168, Jordaan
- 020 625 2041
- Daily 4–11:30
- www.vliegendeschotel.com
- 10

Winkel €
A popular café on Noordermarkt, and a great spot for people-watching during the day when shoppers congregate.
- Noordermarkt 43, Jordaan
- 020 623 0223
- Closed Sat
- 3, 10

EASTERN CANALS

Café De Fles €€
Cosy bar located in a cellar with long wooden tables, serving tapas, meat, fowl and fish. Entrance is via Prinsengracht 955.
- Vijzelstraat 137, Grachtengordel
- 020 624 9644
- Sun–Thu 4pm–1am, Fri–Sat 5pm–2am

- www.defles.nl
- 16, 24, 25

Golden Temple €
Indian, Mexican and Middle Eastern dishes presented in an imaginative menu, served in an atmospheric and colourfully decorated restaurant.
- Utrechtsestraat 126, Grachtengordel
- 020 626 8560
- Dinner only
- www.restaurantgoldentemple.nl
- 4

Hemelse Modder €€
Traditional fresh ingredients are used in the delicious vegetarian dishes served here. The desserts are superb and the atmosphere is relaxed.
- Oude Waal 11, Centrum
- 020 624 3203
- Tue–Sun 6–10
- www.hemelsemodder.nl
- Nieuwmarkt

Indrapura €€
Popular Indonesian restaurant furnished in colonial style. Exceptional *rijsttafel* and a special wine list which is suited to the strength of the spicy dishes, make for a great meal.
- Rembrandtplein 40–42, Grachtengordel
- 020 623 7329
- Dinner only
- www.indrapura.nl
- 4, 9, 14

Pasta E Basta €€
Italian favourites and plenty of pasta in pleasant surroundings. The fun atmosphere is enhanced by the singing bartenders.
- Nieuwe Spiegelstraat 8, Grachtengordel
- 020 422 2222
- Dinner only
- www.pastaebasta.nl
- 16, 24, 25

Piet De Leeuw €–€€

At Steakhouse Piet de Leeuw the house speciality is steak, and also some traditional dishes.

✉ Noorderstraat 11, Grachtengordel
☎ 020 623 7181
🕐 Mon–Fri noon–11, Sat–Sun 5–11
🌐 www.pietdeleeuw.nl
🚌 16, 24, 25

Pinto €€

Located in the Old Jewish Quarter, close to the Joods Historisch Museum, Portuguese Synagogue and Waterlooplein. Menu includes mainly kosher Israeli and French cuisine.

✉ Jodenbreestraat 144, Grachtengordel
☎ 020 625 0923
🕐 Sun–Thu noon–10
🌐 www.pinto-restaurant.com
🚌 9, 14

Sea Palace €€

The Sea Palace is easy to spot. Modelled on a Chinese pagoda-style palace, it is a floating restaurant moored in the Oosterdok harbour.

✉ Oosterdokkade 8, Oosterdok
☎ 020 626 4777
🕐 Daily noon–11
🌐 www.seapalace.nl
🚉 Centraal Station

MUSEUM QUARTER

Bagels and Beans €

Choose from all kinds of bagels, delicious muffins and juices.

✉ Ferdinand Bolstraat 70, De Pijp
☎ 020 672 1610
🕐 Mon–Fri 8:30–5:30, Sat 9:30–6, Sun 10–6
🌐 www.bagelsbeans.nl
🚌 Tram 16, 24, 25

Bodega Keyzer €€

An Amsterdam institution since 1903, located next door to the Concertgebouw; specialising in fish and game in season, and Dutch dishes.

✉ Van Baerlestraat 96, Oud Zuid
☎ 020 675 1866
🕐 Daily 11–midnight
🚌 2, 3, 5, 12, 16

Café Américain €

This grand art deco café has been frequented by artists, writers and bohemians ever since it opened in 1902. It remains a popular meeting spot; a look at the interesting interior alone is worth the price of a drink.

✉ Amsterdam American Hotel, Leidsekade 97
☎ 020 556 3107
🕐 Breakfast, lunch and dinner Mon–Fri 6:30am–11:30pm, Sat–Sun 7am–11:30pm
🌐 www.amsterdamamericain.com
🚌 1, 2, 5, 6, 7, 10

Café Vertigo €€

Lunching in the Film Museum's brown café-style surroundings, where dishes occasionally reflect themes from films is a great experience.

✉ Vondelpark 3, Oud Zuid
☎ 020 612 3021
🕐 Daily 10–1
🌐 www.vertigo.nl
🚌 1, 3, 12

Le Garage €€€

Trendy brasserie in a converted garage near the Vondelpark; French regional cuisine at its best.

✉ Ruysdaalstraat 54–56, Oud Zuid
☎ 020 679 7176
🕐 Daily lunch, dinner
🌐 www.restaurantlegarage.nl
🚌 3, 5, 12, 16, 24

De Oesterbar €€

This elegant fish restaurant offers seasonal delights such as herring in May, mussels in June and delicate Zeeland oysters throughout the summer.

✉ Leidseplein 10, Grachtengordel
☎ 020 623 2988
🕐 Daily lunch noon–3:30, dinner 6–11

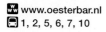
www.oesterbar.nl
1, 2, 5, 6, 7, 10

De Orient €€
For more than 50 years, De Orient restaurant has specialised in *rijsttafel*, with more than 20 different sorts, and several vegetarian options as well.
Van Barleastraat 21, Oud Zuid
020 673 4958
Daily 5–9:30
2, 3, 5, 12

Sama Sebo €€
A Balinese setting complete with batik and rush mats. You can select from their menu to create your own *rijsttafel* combination.
P C Hooftstraat 27, Oud Zuid
020 662 8146
Mon–Sat 9am–10pm
www.samasebo.nl
2, 5

EASTERN DOCKLANDS & IJ HARBOUR

Fifteen €€
Based on the Fifteen London restaurant concept created by famous British chef Jamie Oliver. Fifteen young non professionals are given the opportunity to cook the Oliver way.
Pakhuis Amsterdam, Jollemanhof 9
010 711 1567
Mon–Sat lunch noon–3, dinner 6pm–1am
www.fifteen.nl
25, 26

Gare De L' est €
Formerly a goods stop for workers transporting meat. The cosy 1901 building has been converted into a pleasant restaurant. Serves a three-course meal for dinner.
Cruquiusweg 9
020 463 0620
Daily 6–10
www.garedelest.nl
22, 43

Koffiehuis Khl Amsterdam €
The former coffee house of the KHL shipping company, serving simple food and drinks, with live music.
Oostelijke Handelskade 44
020 779 15 75
Daily noon–midnight
www.khl.nl
26

De Kompaszaal €
Part of the Loods 6 complex, this is a café-restaurant for lunch, drinks, dinner or high tea. There is live jazz on Sundays.
KNSM-Laan 311
020 419 9596
Tue 11–6, Wed–Sun 11am–1pm
www.kompaszaal.nl
26, 42

Restaurant Jaap Hannis €€
Named after a 1603 defence bastion. Offers a delightful menu that changes regularly.
Borneosteiger 1
020 418 9690
Tue–Sun 4–midnight
www.jaaphannis.nl
43, Cruquiusweg

Silk Road €€
Special live cooking stations with delightful fare from India, Indonesia and Thailand. Adjacent terrace, overlooking the harbour.
Mövenpick Hotel Piet Heinkade 11
020 519 1200
Mon–Sat 6:30–11, Sun 7–11
26

Ristorante Pizzeria Oceano €
Situated in a former boathouse on Borneokade, the building served as a canteen for harbour labourers. The industrial space has been a restaurant since 1999, and was also used as an art studio during the 1970s.
R J H Fortuynplein 29
020 419 0020
Daily 5–11 (also Sat–Sun noon–11)

Shopping

Amsterdam has numerous neighbourhood shopping areas, each with its own personality and character. The major one is the Kalverstraat, one of Amsterdam's busiest shopping streets, which can be very crowded. All kinds of shops, from department stores to small speciality outlets can be found here. It runs south from Dam square. To the north is Nieuwendijk, also a major shopping street. Rokin runs parallel to Kalverstraat, and also has a good mix of stores. Leidsestraat is another main shopping artery. P C Hooftstraat is the trendy boutique area, extending into van Baerlestraat and Beethovenstraat, near Museumplein. Small specialised shops and boutiques are in abundance in and around the Jordaan.

CENTRAL AMSTERDAM

Absolute Danny
Houses erotic clothing and accessories, designed with a touch of class. From catsuits and corsets to jackets and uniforms, it's all available here.
- ✉ Oudezijds Achterburgwal 78
- ☎ 020 421 0915
- 🌐 www.absolutedanny.com
- Ⓜ Nieuwmarkt

American Book Center
Four floors lined with English-language books and magazines.
- ✉ Spui 12
- ☎ 020 625 5537
- 🌐 www.abc.nl
- 🚊 1, 2, 5

De Bierkoning
This store stocks international beers and beer mugs from around the world.

✉ Paleisstraat 125
☎ 020 625 2336
🖳 www.debierkoning.nl
🚋 1, 2, 5, 12, 13, 14, 17, 24

Bonebakker
The Netherlands royal jeweller is one of the city's oldest and houses a varied range of fine watches and silverware. You'll find watches by Piaget, Corum, Chaumet, Cartier and Jaeger-leCoultre, and dazzling silver and gold tableware.
✉ Rokin 88-90
☎ 020 623 2294
🖳 www.bonebakker.nl
🚋 4, 9, 14, 16, 24, 25

Condomerie
The world's first specialist condom shop with a wide variety of products. Fun shopping with a serious message about safe sex and sexual hygiene.
✉ Warmoesstraat 141
☎ 020 627 4174
🖳 www.condomerie.com
🚋 4, 9, 14, 16, 24, 25

Den Haan & Wagenmakers
Traditional fabrics, tools and gadgets for quilt-makers. The quality of their cotton chintz (a quilting fabric based on antique Dutch manuscripts) is excellent.
✉ Nieuwezijds Voorburgwal 97–99
☎ 020 620 2525
🖳 www.dutchquilts.com
🕐 Tue–Sat 10–5
🚋 1, 2, 5, 13, 17

Gastronomie Nostalgie
This shop is a must-visit. It specialises in antique silver, silver-plated objects, porcelain, glass and crystal – the kind of tableware used in the charming settings of chic hotels.
✉ Nieuwezijds Voorburgwal 304
☎ 020 422 6226
🖳 www.gastronomienostalgie.nl
🚋 1, 2, 5

Geels En Co
The oldest coffee-roasting and tea-trading company in the country. Enjoy your coffee in a traditional setting surrounded by the aromatic smell of caffeine.
✉ Warmoesstraat 67
☎ 020 624 0683
🖳 www.geels.nl
🚋 4, 9, 14, 16, 24, 25

Head Shop
Operating since the 1960s, this store offers excellent smoking related products including bongs, water pipes, vaporisers, grinders and much more.
✉ Kloveniersburgwal 39
☎ 020 624 9061
🖳 www.headshop.nl
Ⓜ Nieuwmarkt

Hester Van Eeghen
This is the place to shop for Italian made and Dutch designed handbags, wallets and other leather accessories in innovative styles, shapes and colours.
✉ Hartenstraat 37
Ⓖ 020 626 9212
🖳 www.hestervaneeghen.com
🚋 13, 14, 17

Holland Gallery De Munt
Houses souvenirs, miniature ceramic canal houses, costumed dolls, traditionally decorated wooden boxes and trays. It also stocks porcelain antique Delftware, Royal and Makkumer pottery and traditional tiles.
✉ Muntplein 12
☎ 020 623 2271
🚋 4, 9, 14, 16, 24, 25

H P De Vreng
Celebrated wine and spirits establishment, producing fine liqueurs and *jenever* since 1710. Creates Dutch liqueurs and gins according to the old-fashioned methods.
✉ Nieuwendijk 75
☎ 020 624 4581
🚋 1, 2, 5, 6, 13, 17

Magna Plaza

Amsterdam's most luxurious shopping mall, in a spectacular neo-Gothic building. There is a wide variety of distinctive stores here including Villeroy & Boch; Sissy Boy Home and Fashion Decoration; Tolhuysen; Ordning & Reda (Swedish paper merchants); fashion boutiques like Björn Borg, Velvet, Replay, and much more.

✉ Nieuwezijds Voorburgwal 182
☎ 020 626 9199
🅆 www.magnaplaza.nl
🚋 1, 2, 5, 13, 14, 17, 20

Metz & Co

One of the city's most stylish department stores featuring expensive gifts and designer furniture. The delightful café on the top floor is popular for high tea and offers great views of the city.

✉ Leidsestraat 34–36 / corner of the Keizersgracht
☎ 020 520 7020
🅆 www.metz-co.nl
🚋 1, 2, 5

Negen Straatjes

The "Nine Streets" is a wonderful shopping area located along the streets between the main canals from Singel to Prinsengracht, between the Dam and the Blomenmarkt. With 190 unique specialist boutiques, vintage clothes, art galleries, jewellers, gift shops, specialist businesses and plenty of great bars, cafés and restaurants this is the place to be.

🅆 www.theninestreets.com
🚋 4, 9, 14, 16, 24, 25

Oilily

A globally marketed Dutch fashion label selling their own colourfully patterned, bright and cheerful clothing for children and women.

✉ Singel 457 (Kalvertoren)
☎ 020 422 8713
🅆 www.oilily-world.com
🚋 1, 4, 9, 14, 16, 24, 25

Oscar

Popular shoe store housing everything – from the outrageous to sublime, from glittery killer-heeled stilettos to sleek thigh-high boots.

✉ Nieuwendijk 208–210
☎ 020 625 3143
🚋 4, 9, 14, 16, 24, 25

P G C Hajenius

Leading sellers of cigars and smoking articles since 1826. Set in an elegant, art deco-style establishment, this store stocks cigars like Havanas and long, uniquely Dutch, hand-made clay pipes seen in old paintings among other things.

✉ Rokin 92–96
☎ 020 623 7494
🅆 www.hajenius.com
🚋 4, 9, 14, 16, 24, 25

Selexyz

This is the largest bookshop in the city, with one floor of computer software. There are also many interesting audio and video titles in stock too.

✉ Koningsplein 20
☎ 020 523 1411
🅆 www.selexyz.nl
🚋 1, 2, 5

Vroom & Dreesmann

V&D department stores throughout the country offer good quality at reasonable prices. Items include clothing, jewellery, watches, perfumes, electronics, leather goods, household goods and more.

✉ Kalverstraat 201–203
🅆 www.vroomendreesmann.nl
🚋 4, 9, 14, 16, 20, 24, 25

Waterstone's

Reliable English-language bookshop plus English newspapers and magazines and good guidebooks selection.

✉ Kalverstraat 152
☎ 020 638 3821
🚋 1, 2, 4, 5, 9, 14, 16, 24, 25

WESTERN CANALS & JORDAAN

Amsterdam Smallest Gallery
Stocks original artwork, including stunning paintings of the city.
- ✉ Westermarkt 60
- ☎ 020 622 3756
- 🚌 13, 14, 17

Arkwrights
The stop for Brits homesick for traditional British fare. Enjoy sausages, bacon, puddings, and even British and Irish beers.
- ✉ Rozengracht 13, (Jordaan)
- ☎ 020 320 0710
- 🌐 www.arkwrights.nl
- 🚌 13, 14, 17

Beadies
Beads galore for creating do-it-yourself jewellery; huge range of vibrant beads of various materials.
- ✉ Huidenstraat 6
- ☎ 020 428 5161
- 🚌 1, 2, 5, 13, 17

Claire V
Beautiful hand-woven silk handbags, evening wraps and accessories, many made by landmine victims in Cambodia.
- ✉ Prinsengracht 234F
- ☎ 020 421 9000
- 🌐 www.clairev.nl
- 🚌 13, 14, 17

Cortina Papier
Stocks fine paper and writing materials, all kinds of notebooks, from plain to leather-bound and hand-made paper.
- ✉ Reestraat 22
- ☎ 020 623 6676
- 🌐 www.cortinapapier.nl
- 🚌 6, 13, 14, 17

Eichholtz
This established delicatessen with Dutch, American and English specialities is a gourmet paradise.
- ✉ Leidsestraat 48
- ☎ 020 622 0305
- 🚌 1, 2, 5

Fifties-Sixties
The hip era of the 1950s and 60s is recalled in a jumble of period pieces including toasters, vacuum cleaners, records, lamps and other mementos.
- ✉ Reestraat 5
- ☎ 020 623 2653
- 🌐 www.fifties-sixties.nl
- 🚌 13, 14, 17

Frozen Fountain
Interiors store with striking pieces and a dazzling showcase from up-and-coming Dutch designers.
- ✉ Prinsengracht 645
- ☎ 020 622 9375
- 🌐 www.frozenfountain.nl
- 🚌 1, 2, 5

Heinen Handpainted Delftware
Delftware plates, tulip vases and beautiful Christmas decorations.
- ✉ Prinsengracht 440
- ☎ 020 627 8299
- 🚌 1, 2, 5, 13, 17

J G Beune
Famous for its chocolate versions of Amsterdammertjes (the street posts that prohibit cars from parking on the pavement) and a mouth-watering selection of sweets and cakes.
- ✉ Haarlemmerdijk 156
- ☎ 020 624 8356
- 🚌 1, 2, 5, 13, 17

De Kinderboekwinkel
This delightful store offers a large selection of interesting children's books, grouped according to age.
- ✉ Rozengracht 34
- ☎ 020 622 4761
- 🌐 www.kinderboekwinkel.nl
- 🚌 13, 14, 17

Kitsch Kitchen Supermercado

Delightfully colourful shop with an amazing mix of global goods including Mexican tablecloths, Chinese pots and pans, Ghanian metal furniture, Indian beaded curtains and much more.

✉ Rozengracht 8–12
☎ 020 622 8261
🌐 www.kitschkitchen.nl
🚊 13, 14, 17

Outras Coisas

Stocks stylish fashion items, lamps and jewellery ranging from traditional designs to contemporary styles.

✉ Herenstraat 31
☎ 020 625 7281
🚊 1, 2, 5, 13, 17

Shirdak

This store stocks a range of unusual and fascinating products from Central Asia. Among the items for sale are exotic textiles, slippers and rugs. If you're having difficulty thinking of that extra special gift, try this shop. Shirdak also sells unique European felt hats.

✉ Prinsengracht 192
☎ 020 626 6800
🌐 www.shirdak.nl
🚊 13, 14, 17

Sissy Boy

Hip, stylish and affordable clothing is available from this popular Dutch clothing chain.

✉ Leidsestraat 15
☎ 020 623 8949
🌐 www.sissy-boy.nl
🚊 1, 2, 5

Spiegelkwartier

Some 100 specialist shops are located along the canals in Spiegelkwartier, selling an amazing array of art objects and antiques.

🌐 www.spiegelkwartier.nl
🚊 6, 7, 10

EASTERN CANALS

Auction Houses

Amsterdam's main auction houses are Sotheby's (De Boelelaan 30; tel: 020 550 2200) Christie's (Cornelis Schuytstraat 57; tel: 020 575 5255) and their Dutch counterpart, Veilinghuis (Auction House) die Nieuwe Zon, Elandsgracht (tel: 020 623 0343). Presale viewings are held which are interesting to see even if you have no intention of purchasing anything.

De Beestenwinkel

All animal themed products from cuddly toys to soft accessories for all ages.

✉ Staalstraat 11
☎ 020 623 1805
🌐 www.beestenwinkel.nl
🚊 4, 9, 14, 16, 24, 25

Concerto

A great store for music lovers with new and used records and CDs and a large selection to suit all tastes. Good for jazz, classical music and 1950s and 1960s hits.

✉ Utrechtsestraat 52–60
☎ 020 623 5228
🌐 www.concerto.nl
🚊 4

Dappermarkt

Market with around 200 stalls selling various goods. Browse through food stuff, domestic appliances, clothes and footwear, flowers, plants and more.

✉ Dapperstraat
☎ 020 6947495
🌐 www.dappermarkt.nl
🚊 3, 7, 9, 14

Eduard Kramer

This store houses old Dutch tiles, the earliest dating from the 1500s; many rescued from old canal houses. Antique ornaments available as well.

✉ Nieuwe Spiegelstraat 64
☎ 020 623 0832

W www.antique-tileshop.nl
🚌 7, 10

Gassan Diamonds
Offers world-class diamonds. You can pick up a diamond from a spectacular range and then have it set in a beautiful piece of jewellery. There are diamond polishing and cutting tours as well.
✉ Nieuwe Uilenburgerstraat 173–175
☎ 020 622 5333
W www.gassandiamonds.com

De Klompenboer
This wooden shoe factory claims to have the city's largest selection of genuine hand-crafted clogs.
✉ Sint Antoniesbreestraat 51
☎ 020 623 0632
W www.woodenshoefactory.com
🚌 1, 2, 5, 13, 17

Jaski Art Gallery
In the famed Spiegalkwartier, this gallery specialises in painting, sculpture, ceramics and graphic art by the CoBrA artists from 1948 to 1951.
✉ Nieuwe Spiegelstraat 29
☎ 020 620 3939
W www.jaski.nl
🚌 7, 10

MUSEUM QUARTER

Museum Shops
Interesting gifts and art books can be found in all the museum shops in this district, as well as high-quality poster reproductions of famous artworks by both Dutch and international artists. Rijksmusem, Van Gogh and Stedelijk have large selections but even the smaller museum shops have unique finds.

Mexx
Top designer boutique of the Dutch label Mexx. Leading French and Italian labels are also available.

✉ P C Hooftstraat 118
☎ 020 6750171
W www.mexx.com
🚌 2, 3, 5, 12

Oger
A top men's wear boutique with a conservative collection. Made-to-measure suits can be ordered.
✉ PC Hooftstraat 75–81
☎ 020 676 8695
W www.oger.nl
🚌 2, 3, 5, 12

Pauw
An exclusive boutique with stylish fashion for the smart set.
✉ Van Baerlestraat 48 & 66
☎ 020 673 1665
W www.pauw.nl

EASTERN DOCKLANDS & IJ HARBOUR

Keet In Huis
Keet in Huis is an original and trendy kids' store with fashion, toys, furniture and lots of other beautiful products for babies.
✉ KNSM-laan 297
☎ 020 419 5958
W www.keetinhuis.nl

Pol's Potten
Furniture, lamps, accessories, tailor-made kitchens and glassware are the goods on offer here. Also some unique products designed by in-house designers.
✉ KNSM-laan 39
☎ 020 419 3541
W www.polspotten.nl

Entertainment

There is certainly plenty to keep you occupied in Amsterdam after you finish your sightseeing. The city is full of entertainment and nightlife, with more than 2,500 restaurants and 1,400 bars and cafés offering a wide variety of refreshments and snacks. Beer is a favourite, with both Dutch and imported varieties being served. Dutch gin (*jenever*) is distilled, flavoured with juniper berries, aged *jong* (young), *oud* (old) and *zeer oud* (very mellow) and always drunk straight. *Bruin* (brown) cafés are so called because of their dark wood walls, reminiscent of interiors in old Dutch paintings. The city also has modern bars with stylish interiors.

CENTRAL AMSTERDAM

Ahknaton

Multicultural youth venue with the funky sounds of hip music like reggae and rap, and salsa dance nights.
✉ Nieuwezijds Kolk 25
☎ 020 624 3396
🌐 www.akhnaton.nl
🚌 1, 2, 5, 6, 13, 17

Amsterdam Marionette Theatre

Traditional puppet shows may be seen here. Wooden actors, in their dazzling costumes, present operas by Offenbach and Mozart.
✉ Nieuwe Jonkerstraat 8
☎ 020 620 8027
🌐 www.marionettentheater.nl
🚌 1, 2, 5, 6, 13, 17

De Beiaard

This bar has a very prominent location where Spui meets Singel. It specialises in beers from around the world. It is worth trying the draught beer matured in different barrels.
✉ Spui 30
☎ 020 622 5110
🌐 www.beiaardgroep.nl
🚌 1, 2, 5

Beurs Van Berlage

Home to the Netherlands Philharmonic Orchestra and Dutch Chamber Orchestra, this is an impressive concert hall.

✉ Damrak 213

☎ 020 530 4141

W www.beursvanberlage.nl

🚊 4, 9, 16, 24, 25

Café Dante

Hip café with a relaxed, informal atmosphere, good menu and a decor with changing art exhibitions.

✉ Spuistraat 320

☎ 020 638 8839

🕐 Restaurant 11–11; Café Mon–Thu and Sun 11am–1pm, Fri–Sat 11am–2am

🚊 1, 2, 5

De Drie Fleschjes

Wooden casks line the interior of the "Three Little Bottles", a delightful tasting house where locals have tasted Dutch gin since 1650.

✉ Gravenstraat 18

☎ 020 624 8443

🚊 1, 2, 4, 5, 9, 13, 14, 16, 17, 24, 25

De Duivel

This hip-hop club opened in 1992 and kept to its roots with rap and hip-hop beats and a very trendy crowd.

✉ Reguliersdwarsstraat 87

🚊 1, 2, 5

De Engelbewaarder

Sunday jazz from 4pm livens up the scene of this tranquil, arty hangout.

✉ Kloveniersburgwal 59

☎ 020 625 3772

🚊 1, 2, 5, 13, 14

De Heeren Van Aemstel

A vibrant café where you can unwind and enjoy live music, great jazz sessions and hip cover bands.

✉ Thorbeckeplein 5

☎ 020 620 2173

W www.deheerenvanaemstel.nl

🚊 4, 9, 14

Hoppe

A popular brown café, named after the famous Dutch gin. There are two bars, one serving beer and the other gin from the barrel.

✉ Spui 18–20

☎ 020 420 4420

🕐 Sun–Thu 8am–2pm, Fri–Sat 8am–2pm

W www.cafe-hoppe.nl

🚊 1, 2, 5

De Jaren

This is the largest café in the city and offers a spacious ground-floor café and an international reading-table. It also has a pleasant restaurant with a salad bar on the first floor. You can also enjoy a superb canal view from the terrace overlooking the Amstel.

✉ Nieuwe Doelenstraat 20–22

☎ 020 625 5771

🚊 4, 9, 14, 16, 24, 25

Ministry

A trendy and classy café-cum-nightclub with special ladies nights and VIP evenings. The atmosphere is intimate.

✉ Reguliersdwarsstraat 12

☎ 020 623 3981

🕐 Wed–Sun 11pm–5am

W www.ministry.nl

🚊 1, 2, 4, 5, 9 14, 16, 24, 25

Odeon

This recently refurbished, converted 17th-century canalside brewery has a club on one floor, in what was Amsterdam's first concert hall in the 1830s. There is a stylish restaurant in the Gold Room which is open from Thursday to Sunday, with a DJ after 10pm. The café/brasserie in the cellar is open daily from 11am until 1am. The Concert Hall nightclub plays "credible classics" on Fridays and Saturdays until 5am.

✉ Singel 460
☎ 020 521 8555
🕐 Concert Hall Fri–Sat 11pm–5am
🌐 www.odeontheater.nl
🚍 1, 2, 5

Oude Kerk
Regular chamber music concerts and organ recitals are held in this old church, on Saturdays.
✉ Oudekerksplein 23
☎ 020 625 8284
🌐 www.oudekerk.nl
🚊 Nieuwmarkt

WESTERN CANALS & JORDAAN

Alto Jazz Café
A very fine jazz and blues venue, one of the city's best. The live music is great but the drinks are a tad expensive.
✉ Korte Leidsedwarsstraat 115
☎ 020 626 3249
🌐 www.jazz-cafe-alto.nl
🚊 1, 2, 5, 7, 10

Brasil Music Bar
Brazilian bar with live salsa and plenty of dancing on Wednesday nights from 11pm to 4am.
✉ Lange Leidsedwarsstraat 70
☎ 020 626 1500
🌐 www.brazilmusicbar.com
🚍 1, 2, 5

Felix Meritis
An important avant garde dance and drama venue, and home to the Felix Meritis experimental theatre company.
✉ Keizersgracht 324
☎ 020 626 2321
🌐 www.felixmeritis.nl
🚍 13, 14, 17

Het Molenpad
An old-fashioned brown café. On the canalside terrace you can while away the hours and catch some sun.

✉ Prinsengracht 653
☎ 020 625 9680
🌐 www.goodfoodgroup.nl
🚍 1, 2, 5

Papeneiland
The oldest bar in the city operating since 1641, has retained its old-world charm with panelled walls, blue-and-white tiles, candles and benches.
✉ Prinsengracht 2
☎ 020 624 1989
🚍 1, 2, 5, 13, 17

EASTERN CANALS

Backdoor
Enjoy super sounds in this dance club from R&B, disco, soul, funk and weekly retro-theme nights.
✉ Amstelstraat 32
☎ 020 620 2333
🕐 Thu–Sat 11pm–4am
🚍 4, 9, 14

Escape
Feel the beat and join the weekend crowds at Amsterdam's largest disco. With a capacity of 2,000 and a dazzling light show which complements the superb sound system, this place is great to let your hair down and shake out the cobwebs.
✉ Rembrandtplein 11
☎ 020 622 1111
🕐 11pm–4am (also Fri–Sat until 5am)
🌐 www.escape.nl
🚍 4, 9, 14, 20, 24

Herberg Hooghoudt
In this perfectly restored tavern, traditional stoneware *jenever* bottles line the walls. There is a great selection of dishes on the dinner menu.
✉ Reguliersgracht 11
☎ 020 420 4041
🕐 Tue–Sat 4–midnight
🌐 www.hooghoudtamsterdam.nl
🚍 4, 9, 24, 25

Koninklijk Theater Carré

The Royal Theatre plays host to long-running international musicals, revues, cabaret, and the much loved annual Christmas circus.

- ✉ Amstel 115–125
- ☎ 0900 252 5255
- 🌐 www.theatercarre.nl
- Ⓜ Weesperplein

Rain

Rain is a balance of visual and auditory excitement mixing good food, classy cocktails and late-night dancing in chic surroundings.

- ✉ Rembrandtplein 44
- ☎ 020 626 7078
- 🕐 Sun–Thu 6pm–2am, Fri–Sat 6pm–4am
- 🌐 www.rain-amsterdam.com
- 🚋 4, 9, 14, 20, 24

Royal Café De Kroon

Built in 1898, the Crown has been restored to its former grandeur. It encloses a balcony on the first floor, a street side terrace and offers a lunch and dinner menu.

- ✉ Rembrandtplein 17
- ☎ 020 625 2011
- 🌐 www.dekroon.nl
- 🚋 4, 9, 14, 20, 24

MUSEUM QUARTER

'T Blauwe Theehuis

The Blue Teahouse is a 1930s pagoda-like structure and popular lunch spot in Vondelpark, with a large terrace. A fun place to people-watch. There is a stylish bar upstairs with a DJ on Friday evenings.

- ✉ Vondelpark 5
- ☎ 020 662 0254
- 🌐 www.blauwetheehuis.nl
- 🚋 1, 3, 12

Boom Chicago

Boom Chicago is a mix of hilarious sketches and pure improvisation in English and the city's best comedy club.

- ✉ Leidseplein 12
- ☎ 020 423 0101
- 🌐 www.boomchicago.nl
- 🚋 1, 2, 5, 6, 7, 10

Bulldog Palace

Flagship of the Bulldog chain of bars and smoking coffee shops, it also sells Bulldog products. Downstairs is a pleasant smoking coffee shop.

- ✉ Leidseplein 15
- ☎ 020 627 1908
- 🌐 www.bulldog.nl
- 🚋 1, 2, 5, 6, 7, 10

EASTERN DOCKLANDS & IJ HARBOUR

Bim Huis Jazz

Jazz at its best – international talent, improvisation sessions and smooth hot sounds make this a great venue.

- ✉ Piet Heinkade 3
- ☎ 020 788 2188
- 🕐 Mon–Sat noon–7
- 🌐 www.blmhuis.nl
- 🚋 26

Panama

This former port building has been transformed into one of the hippest spots in the city. Enjoy a contemporary nightclub, theatre shows, live music and popular club evenings as well as a trendy dance studio.

- ✉ Oostelijke Handelskade 4
- ☎ 020 311 8686
- 🌐 www.panama.nl

11/Restaurant-Bar-Club

There are many innovative and experimental concepts in this constantly changing trendy club. There are 12 video screens and a podium for eclectic sounds. It is located on the top floor of the Stedelijk CS with an incredible view over the city.

- ✉ Oosterdokskade 3–5
- ☎ 020 625 5999
- 🌐 www.ilove11.nl
- 🚋 26

Travel Facts

Amsterdam is one of Europe's top destinations and can be reached easily by air, land or sea. The Netherlands has an excellent public transport system throughout and Amsterdam in particular is easily accessible. Information about exploring the city by foot with special walking routes, on trams, canal boats or by bicycle as well as current entertainment, events and accommodation is provided by official VVV tourist networks. Of course, you can always ask the local residents who are friendly and helpful. Amsterdam is a cosmopolitan, multilingual city, and home to around 190 nationalities. It's enough to follow the direction signs or consult a city map and guidebook to enjoy and discover the cultural delights of this vibrant city of canals.

HOLLAND INTERNATIONAL

ARRIVING

A valid passport is needed to enter The Netherlands. Citizens from European Union countries and some other countries do not need a vis; however, there are exceptions. EU travellers need only show valid identification, but most customs officials prefer a full passport. It is best to check with a travel agent or the Dutch Embassy in your home country (www.minbuza.nl).

Airport

Amsterdam Schiphol Airport is Europe's fourth largest and is located not far from the city centre. It's also one of the world's most modern, clean and efficient airports. Signs are posted in English and Dutch making it easy to find your way. Inexpensive flights from within Europe and direct flights from abroad are readily available, making Amsterdam a popular destination and Schiphol a busy transportation hub. It's also a great place to shop, open 365 days a year (www.schiphol.com).

Train

Train travel provides a direct railway link connecting Schiphol International Airport to Amsterdam Centraal Station, and it is by far the fastest and most convenient way to get to the city centre. Trains run every 10 minutes from platforms 1 and 2 in the main arrival plaza. Railway information for NS Spoorwegen is available at www.ns.nl or www.nsinternational.nl.

Airport Shuttles run by Connexxion bus service depart every 15 minutes serving more than 100 hotels throughout the city, ticket purchase inside the main arrival plaza, (under €20). Some major hotels provide complimentary shuttles for their guests, so do ask beforehand. Taxis and limousines to the city centre are available but expensive (begin at €40).

Boat

Many visitors from the UK use the popular ferry connections:

Stena Line sails between Harwich and Hook of Holland, day and evening crossings take approximately 4 hours (www.stenaline. com). Hull–Rotterdam (Europort) with P&O North Sea Ferries is overnight and takes 14 hours (www.poferries.com) and Scandinavian Seaways or DFDS Seaways sail from Newcastle to Ijmuiden (www. dfdsseaways.com). Ferries also cross to and from Breskens, Belgium.

Channel Tunnel

Eurostar via the Channel Tunnel runs from London Waterloo to Brussels South in 3 hours and 15 minutes and connects from there with trains to the Netherlands (www. eurostar.com).

Car rental

If you intend to travel only within the city it's not worth the expense and hassle of having a car. Public transport or taxis will save you time and cost less. Amsterdam city centre is rather difficult to navigate by car, with its narrow streets, abundance of bicycles, pedestrians and trams. However, car rental services are available at Schiphol Airport, representing all major agencies including Avis, Budget, Europcar, Hertz, National and Alamo. If you do drive, parking the car and taking public transport is advisable, although parking space is a city-wide problem, and it's very expensive in the parking garages. Wheel clamps are used for overdue street-side parking, which is inconvenient and can cost you half a day until it's sorted out.

Check out www.parkeren.amsterdam. nl for all you need to know about getting around the city, from Park & Ride locations to taxis, trams and bicycles, everything is explained. You must be 18 years old with a valid licence to drive in the Netherlands.

CLIMATE

The Dutch love talking about the weather which can vary from hour to hour. The temperatures are mild from April to

September; however, you can expect rain all year round.

Springtime tends to be the driest and the heaviest rainfall occurs in autumn. The summer varies and winds off the North Sea cool the climate. It can be chilly in spring and autumn and in winter freezes occur, though with less frequency than during the days when the Dutch could skate from city to city. Best be prepared with a raincoat and umbrella, and dress in layers.

DRIVING
At intersections without traffic lights, cars coming from the right have the right of way, except when there are a series of painted triangles (shark's teeth) on the road in front of you. Be alert for cyclists constantly, they will often take the right of way, even when they are supposed to stop. Before making a turn motorists must wait for cyclists continuing on, to clear the intersection. Before opening doors, always check in mirrors for passing cyclists.

Roads are in excellent condition, even the small, scenic country roads. The rules of the road are strict with heavy fines for traffic violations. Visitors from abroad should check with their auto club for advice on documentation.

ELECTRICITY
In the Netherlands the voltage is 230, 50-cycle with a two-pin continental plug. British visitors will need to use an adaptor. US visitors will need to buy a transformer or convert equipment.

EMBASSIES, CONSULATES AND HIGH COMMISSIONS
Dutch Embassies and Consulates located abroad and foreign embassies and consulates in the Netherlands are listed on: www.minbuza.nl.
Foreign Embassies in Holland:
Australia: Carnagielaan 4, Den Haag
tel: 070 310 8200;
www.australian-embassy.nl

Canada: Sophialaan 7, Den Haag
tel: 070 311 1600; www.canada.nl
India: Buitenrustweg 2
tel: 070 346 9771; www.indianembassy.nl
Ireland: Dr Kuyperstraat 9, Den Haag
tel: 070 363 0993; www.irishembassy.nl
New Zealand: Carnegielaan 10, Den Haag
tel: 070 346 9324; www.nzembassy.com
South Africa: Wassenaarseweg 40, Den Haag
tel: 070 392 4501; www.zuidafrika.nl
United Kingdom Consulate: Koningslaan 44, Amsterdam
tel: 020 676 4243
United Kingdom High Commission: Lange Voorhout 10, Den Haag
tel: 070 427 0427; www.britain.nl
United States Consulate: Museumplein 19, Amsterdam; tel: 020 575 5309; http://amsterdam.usconsulate.gov
United States Embassy: Lange Voorhout 102, Den Haag; tel: 070 310 9209; http://thehague.usembassy.org

EMERGENCY TELEPHONE NUMBERS

National number for police, fire brigade, ambulance: tel: 112

National number for police only, but no emergency: tel: 0900 8844

ATAS (Amsterdam Tourist Assistance Service): Nieuwezijds Voorburgwal 104–108, tel: 020 625 3246

ATAS provides a special service to assist tourists who are robbed or otherwise victimised while visiting the city.

Amsterdam Politie Hoofdbureau (Police Headquarters) tel: 0900 8844 (for all police departments)

Stephonsonstraat 18, tel: 020 559 3005; Mon–Fri 9:30–3:30; Tram: 7, 10, 17 Elandsgracht stop.

GETTING AROUND

The GVB (www.gvb.nl) provides integrated metro, tram and bus services throughout Amsterdam and its surrounding areas. GVB passes (24-, 48- and 72-hour) allow for unlimited travel on all public transport for the duration of the pass. Passes may be purchased at all major train stations. For an explanation and current fares visit www.vbn-bv.nl/ovinfo.

Trams are an efficient way to get around Amsterdam and run regularly until just after midnight.

City Buses are primarily used to reach outlying suburbs and after the trams have stopped running.

The Metro or Sneltram (tube or underground) is fast and is useful if you need to travel further for some of the sights, or to travel outside the city centre, for example to the Amsterdam Arena area.

The Canal Bus runs every 40 minutes from 9:50am until 7:25pm with 14 stops along three different routes throughout the city. Day passes are valid until noon the next day. All of Amsterdam's major attractions are on the route and historical commentary is provided along the way (www.canal.nl).

The Museumboot (Museum Boat) is a similar concept with stops at Centraal Station, Prinsengracht, Leidseplein, Herengracht, Muziektheater and the Eastern Dock. A ticket includes half-price entry to most city museums.

HEALTH FACILITIES

In the event of injury or illness you may visit the EHBO (Emergency) at any Dutch hospital. Free medical treatment is available to citizens of the EU (with European Health Insurance Card) and some other countries where the Netherlands has a reciprocal agreement. All others are required to pay the full cost of the medical treatment. You are strongly advised to arrange adequate health and travel insurance before departing.

For medical assistance: Doctors Service, Central Doktordienst/Atacom, tel: 020 592 3434; English speakers trained to handle medical emergencies are available.

SOS Help Line: For medical or dental emergencies in Amsterdam: at night, weekends or holidays: tel: 0900 50 3242.

Distress Line: For help coping with a serious personal or emotional problem, or a major crisis, referral to native English-speaking professional counsellors is available: tel: 020 675 7575. ACCESS, Amsterdam tel: 020 423 3217 and The Hague, tel: 070 346 25 25; www.access-nl.org.

INTERNET
There are a number of internet cafés in the city:
Easy Everything, Regulierbreestraat 22, and Damrak 33, 9am–10pm
Cybernet Lounge, Van Woustraat 82, 10am–midnight
Internet Café Freeworld, Nieuwendijk 30, daily 10am–1am
Internet City, Nieuwendijk 76, daily 10am–midnight
For a complete list visit: www.netcafes.com/netherlands

LANGUAGE
Just about everyone speaks some English, although a few Dutch phrases will definitely prove useful.
Some useful websites include:
www.speakdutch.nl
www.learndutch.org
www.taalthuis.com
There are several English periodicals available as well:
Expatica – extensive online resources for everything in the Netherlands; www.expatica.com
Amsterdam Weekly – Award-winning free arts and culture newspaper; www.amstedamweekly.nl
The Holland Times – newspaper is distributed free at many locations; www.thehollandtimes.nl
Dutch News – Everyday at 4 o'clock with the latest news reports online; www.dutchnews.com
Underwater Amsterdam – Bi-weekly street guide to cultural events; www.underwateramsterdam.com

LOST PROPERTY
For all items lost on trains contact Centraal Station, Stationsplein 15, tel: 020 557 8544. Found items are kept for only three days and then get sent to a sorting depot, NS Afdeling Gevonden Voorwerpen, Tweededaalsedijk 4, in Utrecht, tel: 030 235 3923.
For items lost on the tram contact GVB, Stationsplein across from Centraal Station, tel: 020 460 5858; Mon–Fri 9–4:30.

MONEY MATTERS
Holland, along with 12 other EU countries uses the official euro currency available in bank notes of €5, €10, €20, €50, €100, €200 and €500, and coin denominations are €1 and €2; 50, 20, 10, 5 and 2 cents. Banks no longer handle traveller's cheques. Use the GWK offices at most stations (tel: 0900 0566; Centraal Station daily 7am–10:45pm, Sun 9am–10:45pm; Damrak 66, 10am–10pm; Leidseplein 1pm–3pm and 8:30pm–10pm; Schiphol Airport 7am–10pm; Amstel Station 8am–8:00pm, Sat 8:15am–7:30pm, Sun 10am–5pm). You can change your cash as well as make bank transfers via Western Union, among other services. Also at the Bureau de change, Amsterdam Tourist Office VVV (Stationsplein 10; Tel: 0900 400 4040), where there are English speaking staff members on call (€0.55 per minute). However, there is a much higher exchange rate than at the GWK. The post office has good rates; hotels have the most expensive exchange rate.

POSTAL SERVICES
Centraal Station, Oosterdokskade 3, tel: 020 622 8272 and Singel 250256, tel: 020 330 0555; Mon–Wed and Fri, 9am–6pm, Thu 9am–8pm, Sat 10:00am–1:30 pm; www.tpgpost.nl. Mailboxes are orange in colour with TPG logo. Letters or cards for abroad go into the slot named "overage bestemmingen".

TELEPHONE NUMBERS AND CODES
Public phone boxes are green KPN and
Telfort, usually located at stations. Very few
public telephones accept coins. Pre-paid
phone cards may be purchased at stations,
Primafoon store, supermarkets and post
offices. Note: 0800 numbers are free; for
0900 there is a charge which can be quite
high (typically €0.35 to €0.75 per minute).
   Directory Assistance for Numbers inside
the Netherlands: 0900 1888
Numbers outside the Netherlands: 0900
8418
Operator: 0800 0410
Reverse charges call: 0800 0101
Yellow pages: www.goudengids.nl
White pages: www.detelefoongids.nl

TIPPING
Tipping is not obligatory, but is customary
in taxis, restaurants and hotels. By law
all bills include a 10–15 per cent service
charge, to which clients may add a tip if
so desired.
   For porters usually €1 per bag is
acceptable. Allow €1 for taxi drivers
unless it's a long trip (then add more). The
standard for lavatory attendants is €0.50.

TOURIST OFFICES
Amsterdam's National Dutch Tourist Offices
(VVV) are often crowded, especially the two
at Centraal Station. It will save you time
to gather as much information as you can
before your trip.
   Located on Stationsplein 10, in Centraal
Station on platform 2 and on Leidseplein
1; Open: Mon–Sat 8am–10pm, Sun 9am–
5pm; tel: 0900 400 4040;
www.amsterdamtourist.nl.
Other useful websites are:
www.amsterdamtourist.nl
www.iamsterdam.com
www.visitamsterdam.nl
www.goholland.com
www.easterndocklands.com
www.jordaaninfo.com
www.grachten.nl

NBT – Netherlands Board of Tourism
Nederland's Bureau voor Toerisme,
Vlietweg 15, 2260 MG Leidschendam;
tel: 070 370 5705;
www.holland.com.
NRC – Netherlands Reservation Centre for
Advance Reservations:
www.hotelres.nl.
   For a quick guide to what's on in
Amsterdam, up-to-date information,
entertainment listings and to book a hotel:
www.iamsterdam.nl.
   For entertainment related queries and
tickets contact Uitburo (tel: 0900 0191).

USEFUL WEBSITES
www.netherlands.info
www.holland.com
www.expatica.com
www.amsterdamcitytourist.com
www.hollandportal.info
www.thehagueonline.nl

Index

Spotlight On Amsterdam

Acknowledgements

The Automobile Association would like to thank the following photographers, companies and picture libraries for their assistance in the preparation of this book.

Abbreviations for the picture credits are as follows: (t) top; (b) bottom; (l) left; (r) right; (AA) AA World Travel Library.

Front cover (from top left a-k):
(a) rooftops, AA/K Paterson; (b) Magere Brug, AA/K Paterson; (c) Tulips, AA/M Jourdan; (d) bicycles, AA/K Paterson; (e) NEMO, AA/M Jourdan; (f) Zuiderkirk, AA/K Paterson; (g) canal bus, AA/K Paterson; (h) café, AA/M Jourdan; (i) Concertgebouw, AA/K Paterson; (j) AA/M Jourdan; (k) bicycle, AA/K Paterson.

3 AA/A Kouprianoff; 4tl AA/M Jourdan; 4tc AA/A Kouprianoff; 4tr AA/M Jourdan; 5tl AA/M Jourdan; 5tc AA/K Paterson; 5tr AA/M Jourdan; 6/7 AA/K Paterson; 8 AA/M Jourdan; 12t AA/K Paterson; 12cl AA/M Jourdan; 12bl AA/M Jourdan; 12br AA/K Paterson; 13t AA/A Kouprianoff; 13b AA/A Kouprianoff; 15 AA/K Paterson; 16t AA/K Paterson; 16ct Jochen Tack/Alamy; 16c AA/A Kouprianoff; 16cb Foam_Fotografiemusuem Amsterdam © Maarten Brinkgreve 2006; 16b AA/M Jourdan; 18 Bildarchiv Monheim GmbH/Alamy; 19 Bildarchiv Monheim GmbH/Alamy; 20 Bildarchiv Monheim GmbH/Alamy; 21 AA/M Jourdan; 22/23 AA/K Paterson; 24/25 Jochen Tack/Alamy; 26 AA/A Kouprianoff; 27 Martijn Luns. © Bijbels Museum; 28/29 AA/K Paterson; 30/31 AA/A Kouprianoff; 32 Foam_ Fotografiemusuem Amsterdam © Maarten Brinkgreve 2006; 33 Hermitage Amsterdam; 34 AA/A Kouprianoff; 36 AA/K Paterson; 37 AA/K Paterson; 38 AA/K Paterson; 39 AA/M Jourdan; 40 AA/M Jourdan; 43 AA/A Kouprianoff; 44/45 AA/K Paterson; 46 AA/K Paterson; 47 AA/K Paterson; 48 AA/A Kouprianoff; 50 fotofacade.com/Alamy; 52 Bildarchiv Monheim GmbH/Alamy; 53 Danita Delimont/Alamy; 54 AA/M Jourdan; 55 AA/M Jourdan; 56 AA/A Kouprianoff; 57 AA/M Jourdan; 58t AA/M Jourdan; 58ct AA/K Paterson; 58c AA/M Jourdan; 58cb AA/M Jourdan; 58b AA/K Paterson; 60 AA/K Paterson; 61 AA/M Jourdan; 62 AA/K Paterson; 63 AA/K Paterson; 64 AA/A Kouprianoff; 65 Petr Svarc/Alamy; 66/7 AA/M Jourdan; 68/69 AA/A Kouprianoff; 70 Looier Kunst en Antiekcentrum; 71 Looier Kunst en Antiekcentrum; 72/73 Looier Kunst en Antiekcentrum; 74 AA/K Paterson; 75 AA/K Paterson; 76 Neil Setchfield/Alamy; 77 Bildarchiv Monheim GmbH/Alamy; 78 AA/M Jourdan; 79 AA/M Jourdan; 80t AA/K Paterson; 80b AA/M Jourdan; 81 AA/M Jourdan; 82t AA/K Paterson; 82c Richard Wareham Fotografie/Alamy; 82cb Kermitage Amsterdam; 82b AA/A Kouprianoff; 84 AA/K Paterson; 85 AA/M Jourdan; 86 AA/A Kouprianoff; 87 AA/A Kouprianoff; 88 Richard Wareham Fotografie/Alamy; 90 AA/W Voysey; 91 AA/A Kouprianoff; 92 AA/K Paterson; 93 AA/M Jourdan; 94 Bildarchiv Monheim GmbH/Alamy; 95 Richard Wareham Fotografie/Alamy; 96 AA/A Kouprianoff; 97 AA/K Paterson; 98 AA/K Paterson; 99 AA/K Paterson; 100tl AA/A Kouprianoff; 100bl AA/A Kouprianoff; 100br AA A Kouprianoff; 101bl Diamant Museum; 101br AA/K Paterson; 102 AA/K Paterson; 103 AA/K Paterson; 104 Diamant Museum; 105 Diamant Museum; 106 AA/K Paterson; 107 AA/K Paterson; 108 AA/W Voysey; 109 AA/A Kouprianoff; 110 AA/A Kouprianoff; 111 AA/K Paterson; 112 Picture Contact/Alamy; 113 Peter Horree/Alamy; 114/115 AA/A Kouprianoff; 115 AA/M Jourdan; 116 AA/A Kouprianoff; 117 AA/A Kouprianoff; 118 AA/K Paterson; 119 AA/A Kouprianoff; 120t AA/K Paterson; 120ct AA/M Jourdan; 120c Gian Andrea Montanino/Alamy; 120cb AA/K Paterson; 122 Gian Andrea Montanino/Alamy; 124 AA/A Kouprianoff; 125 AA/A Kouprianoff; 127 John Shapiro, courtesy of Khmer Arts; 128 AA/M Jourdan; 130 Richard Wareham Fotografie/Alamy; 131 AA/K Paterson; 132 AA/K Paterson; 133 AA/M Jourdan; 135 AA/K Paterson; 136 AA/M Jourdan; 137 AA/W Voysey; 139 AA/M Jourdan; 140 AA/M Jourdan; 141 AA/M Jourdan; 142 AA/M Jourdan; 143 AA/A Kouprianoff; 144 f1 online/Alamy; 145 AA/A Kouprianoff; 146 AA/W Voysey; 147 AA/K Paterson; 148 Hugo Nienhuis/Alamy; 149 Imagebroker/Alamy; 150 AA/A Kouprianoff; 151 Suzanne Long/Alamy; 152 Tibor Bognar/Alamy; 153 Art Kowalsky/Alamy; 154 AA/M Jourdan; 155 Keren Su/China Span/Alamy; 156 Danita Delimont/Alamy; 157 Andrew Woodley/Alamy; 158 Robert Estall photo agency/Alamy; 159 Peter Horee/Alamy; 160t AA/M Jourdan; 160b Brand X Pictures; 161 AA/A Kouprianoff; 162 AA/ L Dunmire; 166 AA/K Paterson; 172 AA/K Paterson; 178 AA/T Souter; 182 AA/A Kouprianoff; 183 AA/K Paterson; 185 AA/K Paterson; 186 AA/A Kouprianoff; 188 AA/K Paterson

Every effort has been made to trace the copyright holders, and we apologise in advance for any accidental errors. We would be happy to apply the corrections in the following edition of this publication.

The Automobile Association would like to thank all other contributors to this publication.